Whose Degree
is it Anyway?

Whose Degree is it Anyway?

Why, How and Where Universities are Failing our Students

Professor Robert Naylor

PENCIL-SHARP

First Edition published 2007
By Professor Robert Naylor

ISBN 978-0-9556987-0-5

Every care has been taken that all information was correct
at the time of going to press. The publisher accepts no
responsibility for any error in detail, inaccuracy or judgement
whatsoever.

Publishing Project Management by Pencil-Sharp Ltd

Designed and typeset by Pencil-Sharp Ltd

Printed and bound in Great Britain by Polestar Wheaton

Contents

Foreword

Foreword

THIS BOOK STARTED life some six years ago as an attempt to better inform students and their parents of the realities of contemporary life in higher education. Too many students appeared to be making poor choices in their selection of a course and university.

However, the intervening years have seen dramatic and continuous changes in education in the UK, and particularly in higher education. A plethora of new problems and pressures have come into play which are deeply relevant to this book: university fees and their impact on the already uncertain relationship between universities and undergraduates; the impact of the Research Assessment Exercise on university finances, priorities and the quality of teaching; allegations of bias towards or against pupils from particular kinds of school; the legal rights of students in an increasingly litigious society; and of course, the ever-growing enthusiasm of the modern world for organising others into league tables.

All of these issues deeply affect the outcomes of the choices that our students make, and they powerfully implicate all the stakeholders in higher education: academic staff, government, the tax-payer, graduate employers, teachers in secondary education who offer advice on university applications, as well as, of course, the students and their families.

The simple message of this book is that the unique value of our universities and colleges as seats of teaching, learning and discovery is at risk – and universities alone are unlikely to weather the storm. They need help in identifying the priorities necessary to survive as relevant and reputable institutions, with respect both to teaching and to research.

My views expressed in this book are founded on 35 years' experience as a researcher and teacher – life in the academic commons. As a professor of pharmacology with a personal chair in neuropharmacology, I continue to have extensive teaching duties to undergraduate and postgraduate students, mainly in the healthcare professions.

I am deeply aware that the rapid developments in education can quickly overtake a book such as this. With this in mind, and so that the views expressed in the present book can be challenged, a website has been developed and will be placed online (www.whosedegree.co.uk). It is hoped that all stakeholders in the educational world will contribute to the debate as to how higher education can grow and develop for the best.

I would like to express my particular thanks to Professor D.J. Johns, Dr I.L. Naylor and Professor J.R. Purvis who generously gave their time to reading and commenting on the early stages of this book. I also am greatly indebted to the inestimable driving force of Professor Brenda Costall in establishing the Neuropharmacology Research Group and promoting research at the University of Bradford. I am also deeply grateful for the countless hours spent with the research students and research fellows who so enriched the academic experience, and who now hold academic and other jobs in many countries. They were all tremendous fun. And the collaboration with colleagues in industry in drug research across four continents was surely second to none.

Special thanks must also go to the undergraduate students who have been unfailing in their patience and good humour over the author's lapses in presenting lectures at the correct time. Some have remained good friends and provide much of the inspiration to provide good teaching, whatever the human failings of the teacher.

In the tricky search for a publisher for what was likely to be a controversial book, friend and colleague Dr Rehab Aljamal finally located Lord Lucas who supported the vision. James Croft of Pencil-Sharp then took over the publishing role and my immense thanks must be to him; to Caroline Ball, who spent countless hours in redrafting the manuscript; and to Nigel Halliday, for his tireless patience in improving the presentation. My most grateful thanks to all the staff at Pencil-Sharp who have remained committed to the book. Finally, my sincere thanks to Stephen Naylor for constructing the website.

Robert Naylor
University of Bradford
November 2007

Introduction

Introduction

THE OVER-RIDING REASON that students are now persuaded to go to university is to enhance their career prospects. However, surveys show that, given their time again, one in four graduates would choose to go to a different university; six out of ten graduates would consider doing a different course; and only three in five undergraduates believe their current course is good value for money. Given that this reflects dissatisfaction for tens of thousands of students, which may in turn adversely affect their studies or increase drop-out rates, this is of serious concern. Is it the fault of the students? Or of their advisers? Or of the universities? Why do thousands of students (and their parents, who are often now footing the bill) feel short-changed, and why do employers feel that universities are not producing the goods? This book attempts to find out. Has higher education lost its way and, if so, how and where?

The (it now seems) halcyon days of higher education finished in 1981 with savage financial cuts to many universities by government. The universities had no effective defence. Their autonomy, coupled with self-interest, made them, then and now, divided opponents; governments have walked over them at will.

The ascendancy of New Labour in 1997 accelerated the decline. The Government decided that the future functions of universities would be to provide the nation with a knowledgeable and skilled workforce, to encourage the discovery through research of new commercial activities and products, and to act as sources of expertise and support. Higher education is uniquely available to supply all such needs, and universities have generally attempted to comply with government initiatives, such as engaging with local schools and businesses; changing the admissions regulations to advantage applicants educated in state schools; aiming for the goal of taking 50 per cent of all young people into higher education; developing competencies and providing skills-based teaching to undergraduates to ensure literacy, numeracy and skills relevant to the workplace; and developing collaborative projects with industry.

It was more or less assumed in many institutions that the undergraduate students and the teaching function would simply continue as before. There is no evidence that any one person or committee actually sat down to work out the feasibility of the total enterprise, that anyone calculated whether or not this diverse increase in workload could ever be achieved with the precipitous drop in funding per student that also occurred.

Businesses and commercial enterprises start with a business plan. They identify their potential markets, and design and generate income streams. They decide what they can and cannot accomplish within a given resource. To engage in poorly thought-out and diverse activities is usually fatal. The 'progress' of higher education could not have been more different. The Government instructed a dramatic increase in 'product' output and potential markets to be achieved with a declining resource: higher education on the cheap.

But there were additional difficulties for universities in their expanding role. For the different stakeholders in higher education – the Government (and tax-payers), employers, business interests, academic staff, parents and students – have different perceptions of what actually matters in higher education, and these differences create serious tensions.

The outcomes required by government and society are fairly predictable: a decent and *affordable* level of educational provision for those from all sections of society who might benefit from higher education, to the subsequent advantage of society economically and/or socially. But an affordable level of provision and equality of provision do not necessarily equate to quality of provision.

Employers require a reliable 'output' from which they can identify and recruit the most appropriate candidates for their workforce. Local business interests require an increase in skills, commercial activities and expertise.

Within higher education itself there are a number of competing demands. First and foremost, the institutions have to survive financially in an era of declining financial resources, making tough decisions on priorities. The academic staff might believe that higher education should, above all, be about teaching, the inculcation of higher learning and knowledge and the development of critical reasoning and character. Most academics have considered that the traditional academic vocation of teaching, scholarship and research is a privilege; discovery in teaching and research is a joy. But the academic *business* of the university has been the certification of degrees or diplomas to successful students, and without the business there is no outlet for the vocation. Some academic staff see their primary role as advancing knowledge through research and postgraduate provision, thus benefiting the economic and social welfare of the nation. Also, critically, if they do not pursue research, their career opportunities within a university might be zero; they may even lose their jobs. So, at least in prestigious research universities, staff remain focused on personal research for their very survival. Added to this, and increasingly, some universities are admitting more overseas and postgraduate students, to whom they can charge higher fees, which inevitably reduces the number of places for home students. The entire educational enterprise, from a business perspective, could only be considered barking mad.

What did this mean for those all-important stakeholders, the students themselves? What matters to them is that their education should be directly related to the outcome they require. So, if they prioritise getting a 'good degree' as the essential outcome, they would look to the university to give high priority to the quality of the teaching and learning experience. Some parents and students may additionally hope, or even primarily require, an outcome where the reputation of the institution may focus employer interest to provide a preferential entrance to prestigious jobs and social status. Additionally, they may also reasonably expect university to provide a life-enhancing experience. Academic folklore suggests that the university environment should provide a unique and splendid opportunity for young people to meet with students from different social backgrounds and with foreign students from around the world, to form lifelong friendships as well as networking opportunities, and to develop abilities and characteristics to complement the academic qualifications they obtain, a broadening of cultural horizons and the fostering of a more tolerant, informed and interesting society.

However, these expectations may be compromised by the different outcomes required by other stakeholders. Students and parents may also be confused by allegations that universities show bias in student selection with respect to social standing, type of school or A-level grades, and by the apparent inconsistencies in league tables. They may develop a genuine concern about the declining quality of undergraduate teaching and the uncertainty of students' employment prospects.

A university education in some degree programmes still confers an income advantage. However, the dramatic increase in student numbers has not been associated with any obvious increase in the traditional, professional type of employment opportunities or with an enhanced national prosperity. No less than 20 per cent of first-degree students now study for a Master's degree, to distinguish themselves from the flock in the search for jobs.

To persuade so many young people to enter university without establishing the risks lacks integrity. Some universities have been accused of inappropriately encouraging students to enter universities or courses simply to put bums on seats. However, a more likely explanation for bad advice, not merely from universities but also from school teachers and parents, is simply the absence of informed evidence.

The task at hand is twofold: first, to better inform university academic staff and their administrative colleagues of the reality of the student experience and the present limitations of their teaching and learning experience; and secondly, to re-establish the vital importance of teaching in many universities. As Sir Howard Newby, when chief executive of the Higher Education Funding Council for England, sadly had to remind universities: 'We have to reinvent teaching as being a very honourable vocation that needs to be rewarded. Parents and students paying higher fees are not going to be content if all that [fee-paying] money is going into strengthening the research element of universities.'[1]

The message of this book is that it has become dishonest of universities to pretend that they can honourably fulfil the many responsibilities demanded of them. Their resourcing is inadequate to the task in hand. And one group of stakeholders has lost out more than others: the undergraduate students.

Part 1:
Raising the Curtain
on the Realities of
Higher Education

Chapter 1

Higher Education:

A Global Industry

Higher Education: A Global Industry

W<small>E ALL THINK</small> we know a bit about education: we have all been through it, and many of us have seen or are seeing our children through it. We read or hear about it daily in the news and may have groaned about the exam system and falling standards, been sceptical over ministerial pronouncements, and had our say over school and university tuition fees. For most people their concept of 'education' is loosely based on their own personal experience. We imagine it as a network of moderate-sized institutions with a few thousand students and a thousand or so staff. This parochial view hopelessly underestimates the global size and weight of the industry that is now education, and higher education in particular.

During the last quarter-century, education has quietly become one of the world's greatest industries and one of the biggest players in the labour market of virtually every country in the world. In 1970 the number of students in education at all levels throughout the world was calculated at 608,615,000. By 1997, according to figures published by UNESCO two years later, the number had risen by 90 per cent to 1,154,721,000, nearly one in five of the global population.

In the UK, as in other countries such as Japan, the percentage of students going on to higher education began to rise steeply in the 1960s. From a base of less than 5 per cent it climbed by regular increments over the next 30 years to around 20 per cent, and has continued to rise at an even faster rate since. The USA experienced a similar rate of increase, but the rise there began some 40 years earlier, in the 1920s. The earlier start in America provides us with a unique opportunity to determine what are likely to be the consequences in the UK, if we care to look and have the courage to do so.

Important questions arise from this exceptional increase in student numbers:

- Why has it occurred?

- What have been the consequences for academic staff and the quality of teaching in higher education institutions?

- What have been the consequences for students in search of a rewarding university education, a credible degree and future employment?

The rise and rise of the 'knowledge-based economy'

Governments throughout the world, presumably driven by their voters, have long believed that one of the major functions of higher education is to deliver economic prosperity to their nations. For over 150 years this belief has created tensions between the academic world and society. By the middle of the nineteenth century, higher education in the UK had become a training in character and civic duty. In the 1850s Cardinal John Henry Newman, in a volume of lectures entitled *The idea of a university,* defined university traditions as 'the high protecting power of all knowledge and science, of fact and principle, of inquiry and discovery, of experiment and speculation.'[1] He believed that university prepared individuals to 'fill any post with credit, and to master any subject with felicity'. Cardinal Newman died in 1890 and his grave is inscribed: *Ex umbris et imaginibus in veritatem* ('Out of shadows and phantasms into the truth').

In the second half of the nineteenth century, British universities protected their liberal arts traditions and their autonomy from outside interference by introducing new disciplines and by organising the acquisition of knowledge into defined honours degree courses. As expressed by Soffer in his book *Discipline and power*, 'A university education which began with the classics, supplemented for many by history, was expected to train the judgement to recognise the appropriate balance between change and continuity in national life.'[2]

A liberal education, however, was increasingly under challenge from a developing industrial society controlled by politicians and a growing skilled professional sector, who calculated value in economic terms. However, calculating an individual's input, or value, in relation to his or her contribution to the national economy is not clear cut. In the days of an economy largely based on manufacturing it may have seemed straightforward. Taking such a measure today is much less easy. Earnings are frequently used as an indicator, but they are not an accurate guide. How should the £100,000 a week that a football player may receive be related to the national economy, or the £100,000 a year salary of a government minister? What indeed, is the value of a teacher, or a janitor, or anyone else?

Nevertheless, in the economics of the late twentieth and early twenty-first centuries, frequently described as 'competitive', 'globalised' or 'free market', education, and particularly higher education, has come to be perceived as an essential precondition to national financial success. Indeed, the belief in the great importance of education to a nation's financial health has become enshrined in the cliché 'the knowledge-based economy'. In one sense, this has been an advantage. It has ensured that higher education is perceived as uniquely important in providing the three critical elements for commercial success:

- a knowledgeable and skilful workforce;

- the discovery through research of new commercial activities and products;

- a source of valuable advice for local and national commercial endeavours.

The actions and comments of UK governments reflect just how deeply these beliefs are held. In 1995 the Conservative government merged the departments of education and employment to create the Department for Education and Employment (DfEE), and in a speech in February 2000 the Labour Secretary of State for Education and Employment, David Blunkett, said: 'The power houses of the new global economy are innovation and ideas, skills and knowledge. These are now the new tools for success and prosperity as much as natural resources and physical labour power were in the past century.'[3]

This followed the views of Charles Leadbeater, a policy adviser to Tony Blair and the major author of the Department of Trade and Industry's 1998 policy White Paper, *Building the knowledge-driven economy*:

> The generation, application and exploitation of knowledge is driving modern economic growth. Most of us make our money from thin air: We produce nothing that can be weighed, touched or easily measured. Our output is... in principle at least, to... be organised around people and the knowledge capital they produce. Our children will not have to toil in dark factories, descend into pits or suffocate in mills, to hew raw materials and turn them into manufactured products. They will make a living through their creativity, ingenuity and imagination.[4]

This was echoed in a major policy statement from the prime minister, Tony Blair, the following year:

> Our number one priority for investment is education...
> Brainpower, skills and flexibility... are the key to

competitiveness. For the nation as a whole, it means shifting from a low skill average to a high skill average, and away from an economy built on mass manual labour, with little premium on higher skills.[5]

It was not only governments that were encouraging expansion. Throughout the 1990s the Confederation of British Industry (CBI) was arguing for a 50 per cent participation by young people in higher education by 2010:

> Higher education is a prime source of highly skilled people, a key contributor to a dynamic economy and central to the future competitiveness of UK business... levels continue to lag behind the achievements of some of the UK's major international competitors and the gap must be narrowed to avoid losing competitive advantage.[6]

So the rationale of UK (and other) governments and industry to persuade an increasing number of people to enter higher education was clear. The future prosperity of the nation was at stake. The motivation was fear of failure to keep up. All governments were on the same competitive ladder (or merry-go-round?) But the serious downside to these initiatives is immediately obvious: no government appeared to have the courage to *fund* the dramatic expansion of higher education from general taxation. The deterioration in the existing quality of educational provision was predictable.

More for less

The depth of the problem can be illustrated by a simple analogy. Consider for a moment what would happen if a family doctor with a practice of 4,000 patients were required, without any further increase in resources, to look after 8,000 patients. If the consultation time with the list of 4,000 patients had previously been, say, seven minutes per patient, would the doctor be able to expend as much time and the same degree of care on each of 8,000 patients? Would we not be concerned if this had happened to academic staff in higher education? But in fact the number of UK students increased from 400,000 not to 800,000 but to 2,000,000 – no less than a five-fold increase!

Unfortunately this is only part of the picture. Consider whether the doctor could maintain the required degree of professional care if, at the same time that patients were dramatically increasing in number, resources were being reduced: fewer facilities, fewer nurses, fewer secretaries and fewer support staff. In higher education in the UK resources have dwindled by up to 35 per cent.

There remains one final consideration. Having dramatically increased the doctor's responsibilities, would it be sensible for the Government then to reduce the said doctor's salary relative to those of comparable professional groups by about 30 per cent? What would this do to motivation and morale? Until the 1960s university academic staff were paid at a rate broadly comparable to that of other professional groups. Then, year on year, and especially through the inflationary years of the 1980s, their salaries fell further and further behind. At the end of 1999, David Triesman, general secretary of the Association of University Teachers announced: 'Salaries in higher education have increased in real terms by a mere 1 per cent since 1981, whereas the average real-terms increase for all non-manual workers is nearly 40 per cent.'[7]

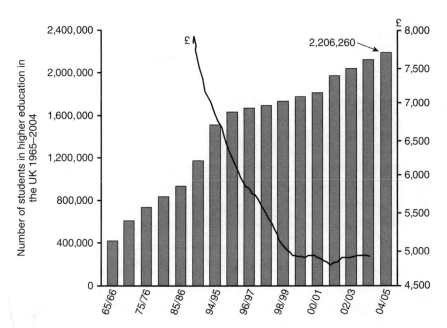

Figure 1.1   The increase in Britain's student numbers in higher education since the mid-1960s and the decline of spending per FTE student between 1989 and 2003 (2001–02 prices, England).

Source: DFES provisional 2002–03, planned from 2003–04.

Many academic staff deplore the fact that the status of their profession has been compromised. Being asked to present lectures to up to 300 (or sometimes even more) students drawn from perhaps several different courses, with different entry-level qualifications and priorities, presents a serious challenge for even an experienced lecturer. They must engage the interest of a highly diverse group of students while maintaining discipline over a minority of uninterested participants. This daunting scenario may even make younger lecturers question their career choice. Meanwhile, students have every right to complain at such facilities.

University bureaucracies that design these 'learning environments', presumably on the basis of 'cost-effectiveness', appear indifferent to the students' fate. Certainly, they are generally indifferent to the fate of the lecturer. Similarly but even more seriously, it may also become a cost-effective exercise to reduce or abolish small-group tutorials or seminars, or to reduce the quantity of student work that academics mark and provide feedback on. Chapter 6 explores in more detail the repercussions of this combination of increased numbers and reduced resources, including its effects on students, staff and higher education as a whole.

A reality check: 'Out of shadows and phantasms into the truth'

No one can seriously doubt the role played by universities in the inculcation of knowledge and skills through teaching and through new discoveries made in the course of research. But that is very different from concluding that graduate employees are in short supply, or that continued economic growth requires more and more highly skilled graduate students.

Indeed, while the growth in student numbers is a global phenomenon, in the UK at least it was not in response to any major increase in the economy's need for graduates. As we shall see in Chapter 10, numbers within the traditional professional occupations have remained fairly constant. The increased numbers of graduates appear to have been recruited into jobs that require them to have additional skills or assimilated into jobs previously filled by those less qualified.

It is time for a reality check. Is it credible that all over the world young people, with the financial support of their parents and families, are entering higher education simply to support national prosperity? Philanthropy has its limits! Surely, those who are making this considerable investment of both time and money in higher education are expecting it to be closely linked to personal gain. They must believe strongly that higher education brings personal benefits, financial or otherwise. As Alan Ryan, warden and tutor in political philosophy at New College, Oxford, notes:

> The differential between school-leavers and degree holders remains obstinately high… So, if you are a prospective student, no matter how little pleasure you get from academic work, no matter how dreary the courses, how boring the teachers, how grotty the housing and bar, you're getting a bargain. A wage differential of 40 per cent over a working lifetime is a good rate of return on your investment. But that doesn't show that it all makes sense, nationally speaking.[8]

So a university education is the high road to greater personal economic success (of which more in Chapter 10). But, like many, Alan Ryan seems to question the validity of the argument that the *national* economy requires more graduates.

In the twenty-first century is a university education the essential precondition for success in the 'knowledge-based economy'? In her insightful book *Does education matter? Myths about education and economic growth* (2002), Professor Alison Wolf studies the possible relationship between university research and economic productivity, and raises some serious doubts. She points to the example of France, where scientific research is concentrated in the Centre National de la Recherche Scientifique, a public-sector institution with interests ranging from physics and chemistry to informatics and the social sciences. She also focuses on Japan, which has looked to commercial rather than academe-based research to achieve its phenomenal growth.

However, many politicians and governments have been almost mesmerised by the way that scientific fallout from the top research universities appears to have bettered the national economy in the USA. But is the performance of the university sector directly linked to the betterment of a national economy or essential to it?

Experiences from across the Atlantic

The idea of education having a role in national economies received scant attention before the 1960s. But in 1962, in an attempt to delineate the various factors contributing to economic growth, a series of landmark publications claimed that education had accounted for some 23 per cent of the growth in total national income and 42 per cent of the growth in per capita income in the US from 1929 to 1957.[9] They argued persuasively that increases in the quality of human resources and education were major sources for economic growth.

There was no hard sell. Economists and sociologists were receptive; people were seduced by the ethos of an educational–economic imperative and US education ranked supreme as a vital social structure. This ethos found expression in President Kennedy's social programmes against poverty and unemployment, and particularly against the educational deficiencies in low-income groups. The ideas had some merit and few would doubt that education contributes importantly to economic and social growth. But within such generalisations lay inconvenient truths.

The great increase in numbers of students in higher education in America had commenced some years before. As early as 1949 Seymour Harris, who was professor of economics at Harvard at the time, advised in his book *The market for college graduates*: 'A large proportion of the potential college students within the next twenty years are doomed to disappointment after graduation, as the number of coveted openings will be substantially less than the numbers seeking them.'[10] Robert Hutchins, president of the University of Chicago from 1929 to 1945, concluded in *The University of Utopia* (1964), a book intended to promote independent thought and liberal education: 'Industrialisation seems to charm people into thinking that the prime aim of life and hence of education is the development of industrial power.'[11]

In the early 1970s Professor Ivar Berg, a sociologist, critically examined the widely held belief that education was closely related to the health of the US economy at large. In his book *Education and jobs: the great training robbery* (1973), he highlighted investigations carried out under the Conservation of Human Resources Project of Columbia University in the 1960s.[12] The thrust of these was to emphasise the extent to which the focus of the American economy was being transferred from the production of goods to the production of services, and to look into the economic and social institutions that constitute the framework within which people can earn their living.

During this period academic economists and public leaders were developing a new ideology. They believed that the key to economic development was increasing expenditure on education, and that improving the quality of labour would lead to productivity increases. The motto throughout the nation, from the president downwards, was: 'Education pays; stay in school.'[13]

In an incisive analysis Professor Berg identified that the critical point was not whether graduates are able to make more money than non-graduates, but whether their higher earnings are a reflection of more education and training or of factors other than diplomas or degrees. Unequivocal and detailed studies of data obtained from the armed services and federal civil service proved overwhelmingly that the critical determinants of performance are *not* increased educational achievement but rather experience and personality characteristics of aptitude.

Data therefore was already available over 40 years ago to make us question any simple relationship between academic achievements and economic growth. However, the experience in Britain has followed a similar pattern to that of the USA: the move from a manufacturing to a knowledge economy; political and economic policies based on the firmly held belief that a more highly educated workforce would lead to greater productivity; and the expansion outwards and downwards of what constitutes 'graduate territory' in jobs and careers.

In summary

In the light of this brief overview of history and economics, we can begin to answer the three questions identified at the beginning of the chapter. The dramatic increase in student numbers in higher education occurred because higher education was believed to hold the key to a nation's successful entry into a 'knowledge-based economy'. There is no evidence that entry into a knowledge-based economy was or is dependent on increasing the number of students entering higher education. There is, however, evidence that increasing the number of students entering higher education without increasing resources reduces

- the quality of their teaching and learning; and
- their prospects for appropriate employment.

This role of education as an economic driver has had many repercussions, not least for students themselves. One of these, which we shall look at next, is the profound effect the knowledge economy and all it entails has had on universities themselves, how they perceive themselves and how they are run.

Chapter 2

The Corporatisation of Universities

The Corporatisation of Universities

CHAPTER 1 HIGHLIGHTED TWO trends which played an important role in the decline in quality of higher education now offered to our students: a dramatic, externally imposed increase in the number of students, and a reduction in their financial support. But for over a hundred years many academics have believed that there are even greater threats to the purpose of universities, which may erode and finally destroy the entire higher educational enterprise.

In his seminal book *The idea of the university* (1946) the philosopher Karl Jaspers described the university as 'a community of scholars and students engaged in the task of seeking the truth'. Is this how universities are regarded today? Is it, indeed, how they see themselves?

Communities of scholars or makers of money?

Towards the close of the nineteenth century, the idea that the object of higher education in the UK was an understanding of knowledge itself, the ideal of a liberal education, was being questioned. There was increasing agreement, based partly on self-interest, that higher education must promote a national elite. The Oxford Appointments Board was begun in 1892 and, with business backing, in 1899 the Cambridge Appointments Association was founded. They were placing between 8 and 14 per cent of their clients in business and industry, a modest beginning to external pressures to move with the times.

In addition, although reluctant to bring the 'lower classes' into their universities, Oxford and Cambridge, through extension teaching, began to reach out to the less privileged who wanted to contribute to national life.[1]

In America also there were concerns within the university community that the commercial world and the introduction of its practices into academia might adversely affect their purpose. In 1909 a Harvard alumnus, John Chapman, complained that 'the men who control Harvard today are very little else than businessmen, running a large department store which dispenses education to the millions'.[2] The leading educational authority of his period, Abraham Flexnor, castigated Harvard for creating a business school: 'Modern business does not satisfy the criteria of a profession; it is shrewd, energetic, and clever, rather than intellectual in character; it aims – and under our present social organisation must aim – at its own advantage rather than at noble purposes within itself.'[3]

Later, Peter Caws was to go further, suggesting in 'Design for a university' (1970) that 'trustees, presidents, deans, registrars, secretaries, janitors, and the like are not, strictly speaking, part of the university at all. They are ancillary to the real business of the university, and only the supplanting of the community model by the corporation model has put them in their present dominant position.'[4] The sociologist Stanley Aronowitz more recently observed: 'The learning enterprise has become subject to the growing power of administration, which more and more responds not to faculty and students but to political and corporate forces that claim sovereignty over higher education.'[5]

So the influence of the commercial world on the purpose and conduct of higher education has been interpreted in a negative manner by the academic community for over a century. Is this merely a reluctance on the part of the academic community to subjugate their influence and power to a greater good? Or is concern justified, and is there a mounting utilitarianism that may destroy higher education?

Supportive evidence for the latter view comes from a surprising source. The Council for Industry and Higher Education in the UK, notwithstanding its focus on skills acquisition, has expressed just this concern. In their report *Higher education and the public good* in 2004 they call for greater attention to the 'key virtues' of universities to restore a sense of purpose amongst students and staff:

1. Universities must be more vigilant and robust in defence of their key virtues.

2. Universities should pay more attention to the values that shape, and are shaped by, the student experience.

3. Universities should equip people and society with the moral and ethical tools to make informed decisions.

4. Universities' engagement requires greater attention to the more abstract to quantify and evaluate.[6]

'The academic executive and all his works'

Towards the end of the twentieth century, nations woke up to the fact that universities held in their hands the three ingredients essential for national prosperity: scientific advances that can translate into successful new products, expert knowledge and highly trained personnel. These assets secured them a particularly powerful role. This was very good news for the universities.

Then came the relatively good news: a climate of entrepreneurship developed in universities, usefully broadening the academic horizon to include at least a passing interest in the real world. The money raised was appreciated by staff and institutions too.

And then the bad news. In the 1970s and 1980s governmental support for higher education declined. As could have been predicted, academic entrepreneurship was encouraged as a serious endeavour to raise additional and much needed financial support. Money was no longer appreciated by the institutions but expected on demand. This may have exacerbated the inherent culture of universities and colleges to compete with each other. But the collision with the market place in a vicious competition in the pursuit of money, prestige and cost-effectiveness, insidiously but inevitably flowed into commercialisation, marketing and corporatisation to make profits from teaching, research and anything else remotely related to campus activities.

And then the very bad news. Many academics believe that the crudity of raw financial power changed the fundamental value of teaching, research and other university-based activities, and also the value of individual members of faculty, who became measured and valued primarily in terms relating to their immediate financial worth. In brief, every activity came to be precisely measured according to the profit made. To the dismay or disgust of some (or most?) academics, markets, management, salesmanship and clever branding have flourished and appear to be supplanting academic vision and values, truth and trust. Maintaining academic communities of scholars and students is simply irrelevant to the market place.

Who was to blame for this desecration of the academic workplace? For the economist Thorstein Veblen the guilty party was already obvious 90 years ago: university presidents and their administrative entourage. The leaders of universities, he observed then, were already attempting to increase the reputation and size of their various institutions and were to be held responsible for inflicting the ethos of the marketplace on reluctant academics. To Veblen the remedy was simple: 'The academic executive and all his works are an anathema and should be discontinued by the simple expedience of wiping him off the plate.'[7]

This somewhat drastic solution (although perhaps pleasing to the academic corpus!) was and remains, however, an incomplete explanation. Is one seriously to believe that the university hierarchy was required to *force* professors to sell their intellectual property for handsome returns, sell their services as teachers, found their own companies and undertake lucrative consulting and other forms of entrepreneurial activity? Reductions in government support for higher education in the 1970s and 1980s may have contributed to the increase in commercial activities, but many academic staff willingly contributed to the ever-broadening academic brief, which was often well paid. It would be unsafe to exclude any within the academy from contributing to the decline in academic standards.

Professor Derek Bok provides one of the most thoughtful accounts of the confrontation between commercialisation and the academic world in his book *Universities in the marketplace: the commercialization of higher education* (2003). Professor Bok has impeccable academic credentials: he is former head of Harvard Law School and has twice served as President of Harvard University. Therefore his perspective comes from both the academic commons and as leader of one of the world's most prestigious research universities. His view, rather more temperate than Thorstein Veblen's, is that those who lead the universities – vice-chancellors, provosts or rectors, principals, presidents and deans – can find themselves caught between a rock and a hard place. They head up large organisations, but are perforce intellectual leaders rather than corporate managers. They may lack the experience of their commercial counterparts, and their successes are not as easily measured: there are no indicators comparable to market share or stock price to determine academic successes or failures. Accomplishments are gauged by, for instance, building academic programmes rather than making greater efficiencies or cost-cutting. With the serious difficulties inherent in measuring the value of research output or how much students are learning, efforts by universities to adapt a corporate model to measure performance or 'manage by objectives' are much more difficult than they are for a business enterprise.[8] Also, as Professor Bok points out, 'The ethos of the university keeps them from earning sums remotely comparable to those of top business leaders.'[9]

On the other hand, he notes, businesses strive continuously to improve the quality of what they do, something he sees little evidence of in higher education:

Very few universities make a serious, systematic effort to study their own teaching, let alone try to assess how much their students learn or to experiment with new methods of instruction... Professors who look down on business would do well to bear this point in mind before dismissing the ways of commerce as irrelevant to the academy.[10]

Many academics would agree with Professor Bok's serious yet balanced views of shortcomings in the quality of the provision and assessment of teaching, and would accept his conclusions:

To commercialise a university is to engage in practices widely regarded in the academy as suspect, if not downright disreputable... Scholars, especially in the traditional disciplines, have deliberately chosen academic life in preference to the ways of commerce, in part because they look upon the search for truth and knowledge as a worthier calling than the quest for material wealth... They fear that money and efficiency may gradually come to have too dominant a place in academic decision making and that the verdict of the market will supplant the judgement of scholars in deciding what to teach and whom to appoint.[11]

It could be argued that the dangers of commercialisation to the conscientious-ness of faculty, or to the moral education of students, or to the trust of the public, are all intangibles and remote. They may never materialise, at least for a long time, so it is easy to overlook them.[12] The following illustrates how innocently the seeds of destruction can be sown.

Sowing the wind...

In 1852 two groups of athletes were persuaded by 'lavish prizes' and 'unlimited alcohol' to row against each other on Lake Winnipesaukee. The two teams came from Yale and Harvard and, seen in retrospect, provided the first intercollegiate sports contest in the United States. The sponsor intended the spectacle to attract the public's attention to the undoubted beauty of New Hampshire, and within the apparent pleasure and innocence of the occasion no one could have predicted that this germ of 'commercialism' in American higher education, linked to intercollegiate athletics, especially football and basketball, would incur such a heavy price.[13]

Winning became all-important. It led to scholarships for promising athletes, professional coaches, training tables, paid recruiters. Sport descended into sporting barbarism – football resulted in 21 deaths in 1904 alone. But it was immensely popular with students and alumni and generated publicity for student recruitment. The quest for money increased: luxury stadium boxes were added to attract corporate sponsors and wealthy patrons; in due course radio and television brought useful additional revenue, followed by athletes adorned with corporate insignia, and so on.

Robert Hutchins, president of the University of Chicago in the 1930s, abolished football at his university and took his institution out of the Big Ten, a remarkable feat by a remarkable man.[14] Harvard's longest serving president (1869–1909), Professor Charles W. Eliot, had also attempted abolition of the sport that had 'become a brutal, cheating, demoralizing game', but he was over-ruled by his governing boards. University presidents of today would find such a manoeuvre virtually impossible. All of them are under unrelenting pressure to raise substantial sums of money every year from many sources simply to maintain their extensive commitments. The public image and the importance of the donors loom large.[15]

But it became apparent that it takes a lot of money to make money. Some football and basketball coaches were making over $1 million a year, far more than most college presidents. Many universities were failing to generate a sensible financial return and, given the intense pressures to win, cheating by coaches, athletics directors and alumni was a serious problem in some colleges. A major, but more insidious, cost has been to academic standards.

... and reaping the whirlwind

Data collected in 1993 revealed that in some selective public universities, members of football and basketball teams were being admitted with SAT scores averaging 237 points below the mean for the class as a whole. It is not unexpected that athletes perform less well academically than their classmates, and their graduation rates are also lower, even though they may receive full scholarships and extensive tutoring to help them with course work. There is also a clear perception that many athletes do not attend college primarily for an education, although it is also recognised that the time they are required to devote to their sport may also detract from the extracurricular activities enjoyed by other students.[16] Thus high-pressure athletics makes it difficult for students easily to obtain either the normal educational or social benefits of attending college.

As far as the universities are concerned, protecting their investments tempts them into ensuring that their athlete 'students' succeed at any price, sometimes going to lengths that can only be described as deceptive or dishonest. This does not enhance a university's reputation in the eyes of its academic students and staff.[17]

In a report to the Carnegie Foundation for Teaching in 1989, Ernest Boyer (who served as the commissioner for education and president of several universities) wrote: 'The cynicism that stems from the abuses in [intercollegiate] athletics infects the rest of student life, from promoting academic dishonesty to the loss of individual ideals.'[18] James J. Duderstadt, former president of the University of Michigan, in his book *Intercollegiate athletics and the American university: a university president's perspective*, asserted: 'The mad race for fame and profits through intercollegiate athletics is clearly a fool's quest.'[19]

How do university presidents justify such policies, described by *Time* magazine as 'an educational travesty – a farce that devalues every degree and denigrates the mission of higher education'?[20] Clearly, justification is not possible, although interested readers may like to read pages 46–51 of Professor Bok's *Universities in the marketplace*, where he summarises the pitiful attempts to do so.[21]

Members of the Ivy League have committed themselves not to give athletics scholarships, not to admit athletes with grades or test scores substantially below the levels of their classmates, and not to schedule games that force students to miss classes. But not all institutions have the private funds and generous alumni of the Ivy League, and losing athletics money is, commercially, not an option.

In brief, the ramifications of the innocent athletic spectacle on Lake Winnipesaukee over 150 years ago have been seen to inflict serious damage on the moral and educational status of the American educational system.

Denigrated by the corporate approach

Alongside the overt commercialism of the sports field, there are sometimes subtle factors of commercialism or corporatism that have led to the purported lowering of standards. This may then in turn affect the reputation of an institution, the academic staff and its leadership and, inevitably, the quality of its teaching, learning and research.

For instance, research has felt the long finger of the corporate touch. In his book *Enemies of promise* (2004) Lindsay Waters, executive editor for the humanities at Harvard University Press, wrote: 'The corporatist demand for increased productivity has drained publication of any significance other than as numbers. Books and papers have come to be merely counted or worshipped – but not read.'[22]

The English academic may be disbelieving that an entire academic community and its leaders may have cravenly capitulated to demands to measure research success by the number of research papers or books published. Must UK academics acquiesce? Well, they almost certainly will – and perhaps some or many already have done. Why does this happen? Some vice-chancellors may perhaps purport to or genuinely believe that such measurements used to assess research success have real authority. But it is the ease of measurement that is so beguiling to the administrative mind: it requires no further effort to think of what the numbers actually mean.

What makes the threat so dangerous is that it is not the barbarians who have penetrated the gates of academe: the enemy is within. It is those who lead universities, vice-chancellors and others, together with senior colleagues in administration and management, who appear quietly confident of their self-destructive actions.

Higher education and the human good, a survey published in 2006, reported that higher education is 'selling its soul', meaning that managerialism, regulation and the drive to get 'bums on seats' is replacing the wider human good of academe. In the survey, edited by Ian McNay, emeritus professor at Greenwich University, and Jennifer Bone, former pro-vice-chancellor of the University of the West of England, almost 80 per cent agreed that academic freedom ('speaking truth to power') was being sacrificed to a culture of 'bully and blame'. The survey, which targeted members of the Higher Education Academy's Learning and Teaching Subject Networks, also found that 72 per cent of academics think higher education has lost its role as the 'conscience and critic of society'. Some 85 per cent agreed that the 'humanity and excitement' have been lost, while 77 per cent said the 'joy of learning, once associated with higher education has been lost to targets and performance measures'.

Bill Rammell, then Higher Education Minister, disagreed:

> The response from this self-selecting survey reads a bit like 'Stop the world, I want to get off.' Investment in higher

education is now increasing whereas previously, for a generation, it had decreased. Higher education is still a critic of society and rightly so.[23]

But his appears a minority view. In November 2006, in an article entitled 'Profs attack managers', 27 professors at Middlesex University were reported as having 'accused managers of "eroding the academic fabric of the institution" and threatening its future'. The professors expressed concern about potential worsening of the student–staff ratio and about the university's 'commitment to supporting and developing research'. The University and College Union's regional official, Jenny Golden, said: 'Our members are moving towards a position where they increasingly have no confidence in the management or governance of the university.'[24]

A heavily corporate approach can result in excluding, or at least reducing the involvement of, academic staff in academic and academic-related activities. Where there is a perceived urgent need to develop a corporate philosophy and administration, democracy seems to threaten a never-ending cycle of faculty debates. Nor is this just a British problem: in Australia a study of the 'enterprise university' revealed that 'without exception the university leaders saw collegial forms of decision-making as an obstacle to managerial rationalities'.[25]

Clearly, it has been less onerous for administrators to avoid the faculty input; the crafted views of the workers at the coalface are an impediment to corporate or political wisdom. We appear to be approaching open warfare. And the warfare has been opened by those leading universities on two fronts, not merely against the academic staff but also against students and parents.

Broken promises

At Leeds University, in a call for a fight against 'unfair' contracts in 2006, students were urged to fight back against one-sided contracts that limited their consumer rights after the university's student union managed to rewrite an 'unfair' accommodation deal. The NUS said it would challenge such contracts in the courts as they unfairly removed students' basic legal rights. Education law expert Jaswinder Gill said the success of the student union in tearing up a 'one-sided' accommodation contract should be an example to all students: 'There is a need for real equality and fairness between students and universities. Universities appear to be going to extreme lengths to widen the gap on equality in their favour, in desperate attempts to halt complaints and claims and to disguise increasingly poor quality education.'[26]

An adversarial relationship between universities and students can be highly destructive to the institution. In October 2006 angry students at Reading University criticised senior management for abandoning a commitment to keep the physics department open. Reading Students' Union issued a statement saying: 'University senior management have gone against the recommendations of a previous exhaustive review that reported that there should be a continuation of the physics department, that additional funding for staff would be committed and that a strong, viable physics presence was key to fulfilling the university's corporate plan.'

Dave Lewis, union president, said: 'Is this announcement in the best interests of students? No. Were we consulted? No. Is there any consistency in decision-making? No. Has the university made a mistake? Definitely.' Ryan Bird, the union's vice-president for education, added: 'While we want to tell students that Reading is where their future lies it was sociology last year, mechanical engineering before that and music the year before. We can't promise students today their department will be open tomorrow.'[27] Such comments are the last thing that any university would wish to see, contradicting the picture painted in their persuasive prospectuses.

In the past few years, there have been worryingly regular reports of similar breaches of promise.

- In November 2004 a 1000-strong demonstration by Cambridge students and supporters protested against the closure of the university's architecture department.[28]

- The same month, it was revealed that proposals were to be placed before a senior tutors committee at Oxford to reduce the number of tutorials in English from eight to four per term.[29]

- A group of angry parents and secondary school teachers prepared to take legal action against Exeter University if it approved plans to close its chemistry and music departments. The campaign group Parents against Cuts at Exeter (Pace) were prepared to mount a court action accusing the university of breach of contract.[30]

A report from the Higher Education Policy Institute (HEPI) in November 2006 found that 13 per cent of overseas students (compared with 9 per cent of UK students) believe they have been misled by claims made in university prospectuses. This has rung alarm bells about the ability to attract students from lucrative overseas markets. Some 9 per cent of the overseas students said they had received 'very poor' value for money, compared to 3 per cent of all respondents. Non-EU and overseas made up about 10 per cent of the 15,000 students who responded to the HEPI survey. Bahram Bekhradnia, director of HEPI, commented: 'There are lessons here that universities need to take very seriously.' The report warns that by failing to meet foreign students' expectations, universities are in danger of 'killing the golden goose'.[31]

These accusations are serious, because they suggest that universities have crossed the line between honesty and dishonesty. Or has the corporate approach and marketing simply blurred the line in the sand? The behaviour of the universities provides a poor example of a duty of care.

The above examples illustrate the costs to reputation that commercialism can bring to an institution. If overseas students believe they have been misled, this implies a serious allegation of misrepresentation. Course closures and the introduction of one-sided contracts also reflect questionable values held by an institution, but in a more definitive and damaging manner. They are clear and definite statements of the moral values held by the institution, and this has serious implications. The illusion of the spoken and written pronouncements of the purported 'excellence' of a university's institutional aims and objectives, mission statements and glossy prospectuses dissolve in the truth of the daily example of their standards of behaviour.

Providing a role model

At the annual conference of the Society for Research into Higher Education in December 2006, which charted changes to academics' jobs and professional identity, it was concluded that the emerging gaps in the outlook of staff from different generations could lead to a splintering of the academy and of academic identity. 'Young academics have never known anything different and accept it as normal,' said Janice Malcolm, a senior lecturer in academic staff development at Kent University. 'For them, being an academic has become much more about getting ahead in their career than advancing knowledge. We have allowed things to fragment around us, and we have not defended universities as major social institutions. We have let ourselves be undermined.' But Cath Lambert, a sociology lecturer at Warwick University, saw hope in the determination of many young academics not to let traditional values die: 'Young academics accept that there are hoops they must jump through; but at the same time they see there are ways of managing the academy that preserve its integrity in providing education for education's sake.'[32]

It may appear that UK universities have forgotten – through financial pressures, ignorance and/or arrogance – the crucial role model provided to staff and students by the daily (and very public) behaviour of the university itself. Will university behaviour change or will we have to wait for the demise of the present establishment? Would a new generation of academic disciples restore a duty of care to those who have placed their trust in universities? The future, as always, is uncertain.

What is at risk?

The public perception of a university has been focused around a community of scholars and students, with each group performing of their best to ensure high standards in teaching, learning and research. There is an *a priori* assumption that the goals of the faculty in both teaching and research are not primarily self-serving: truth and understanding are the key issues, and universities are about different priorities from those of the commercial world. Overall they appear to have enjoyed respect and a good reputation.

Yet, as with any other institution, reputations are fragile assets which, once broken, are difficult to repair. As universities have increased in size, affection for, or at least tolerance of, the institution may be increasingly mixed with concerns. Within the UK and whatever the actuality, universities have generally received a poor press with respect to a perception of their bias or prejudice in the selection of students based on social background (see Chapter 3). In addition, the portrayal in the press of some universities providing 'Mickey Mouse' courses leads to a general feeling of dissatisfaction, a sense that some standards are inadequate. Finally, the deliberate closure of an undergraduate course not merely destroys trust, but creates very real anger among students and parents.

Not all these effects can be directly attributed to the universities themselves. But the sum total of these individual acts, or at least the manner in which they are presented, can be perceived as arrogant or neglectful, which inevitably leads to resentment and distrust. This may in turn lead to questions about academic autonomy and demands for increased regulation of academic standards in the way that is already being progressed for many other professions.

When Sir Colin Campbell, vice-chancellor of Nottingham University, entered into negotiations with the British American Tobacco Company (BAT) to accept funding of £3.8 million to help fund a new 'International Centre for

Corporate Social Responsibility', the decision caused a storm of protest. The use of a single paragraph in the protocol by the Nottingham vice-chancellor to justify taking BAT cash was condemned as 'clever, but cynical' by Gordon McVie, director-general of the Cancer Research Campaign.[33]

Despite this very public PR disaster, a survey of academic trends conducted by the Cardiff Business School reported in 2004 that academics were being pressurised to bring research money in from whatever source, at the expense of what they saw as more important academic research.[34] A £4 million recruitment drive at Royal Holloway, University of London, was launched early to pre-empt similar exercises by other universities and maximise the chances of luring the best academic talent.[35] A major senior-management shake-up at Nottingham Trent University followed a damning Mori poll that showed that a significant minority of staff had no confidence in their managers, with management having placed undue emphasis on embracing the marketisation and commodification of higher education.[36]

These are just a few examples of controversial or questionable decisions or opinions that illustrate what has happened when higher education has appeared to place money before academic values or principles. It can profoundly affect the fundamental values of an institution and, as in war, truth and integrity are invariably the first casualty. Some of the consequences can be surprising.

Reputations are at risk, but so too are academic standards, and lowering these is, in effect, cheating our students. The clear trend for appointments to focus primarily on research instead of teaching is usually driven by an institutional insistence. However, it may jeopardise teaching needs and the quality of student instruction, a corporate folly explored in Chapter 5. Creating even the perception that staff have been appointed for fiduciary reasons will lower faculty morale and diminish the reputation of the institution. The questionable nature of such behaviour may rightly irritate or offend staff, students and parents.

Introducing opportunities for staff to obtain private financial gain in lucrative research or teaching initiatives has always had to be carefully balanced within the departmental research and teaching provision. Some staff have achieved celebrity status on television in splendid historical or scientific documentaries, and individual success must be warmly congratulated within a balanced academic perspective that is welcomed by all staff. Academic staff usually have no difficulty in distributing between colleagues the academic duties of teaching, research and administration: frequently it is welcomed to allow all colleagues to play to their strengths. It is acknowledged that all three functions are vital to keep the ship afloat. All staff must be valued. A small erosion in respect and trust below the waterline will sooner or later cause listing, then finally immersion below the waves. It is so easy unintentionally to undermine a collegiate spirit and trust between colleagues – to destroy the very cohesion that keeps the academic ship afloat – and colleagues who feel devalued are unlikely to be able to give of their best.

Preserving the values that count

David L. Kirp, professor of public policy at the University of California, describes the 'marketisation of higher education' as follows:

> The market and the university make uneasy bedfellows... Embedded in the very idea of the university are values that the market doesn't honour: the belief in a community of scholars and not a confederacy of self-seekers; in the idea of openness and not ownership; in the professor as a pursuer of truth and not as an entrepreneur; in the student as an acolyte whose preferences are to be formed, not a consumer whose preferences are to be satisfied. In crafting policy, the trick is to figure out how to combine the best of both world views, the academic commons and the market place, creating institutions that are successful and principled competitors in the higher education bazaar.[37]

The evidence, generally consistent, shows that academic staff and institutions, driven by corporatism and commercialism, are losing their sense of purpose. This directly affects the quality of teaching and research and the quality of the undergraduate experience. A further and major force is selfishness: some universities will obtain parochial benefit from the financial handouts. Because universities are a divided house – intensely competitive against each other, with a difference in goals and a fiercely protected autonomy – there will be little or no interest by the winners in the fate of other institutions or the consequences to higher education or the nation overall.

If this is a realistic assessment of the developing threat, how do we save the vital functions of teaching and research as worthy endeavours in their own right? It will require active involvement from all those who have a stake in higher education, in particular the academic and administrative staff, students, parents and employers.

Chapter 3

Student Selection:
Do Bias and Prejudice Exist?

Student Selection: Do Bias and Prejudice Exist?

THERE ARE FEW issues that divide the social classes more than the merits of independent versus state schooling. Many parents believe that quality of education will decide their children's fate in life, and make extreme sacrifices to secure their children's education within the independent sector. A pupil working for quality grades at A level sees them as the vital determinant for whether they get into university. News that universities might be biased or prejudiced against the selection of a student on the basis of factors other than academic ability or potential must be the last straw.

Over the last ten years there has been an incessant, almost weekly stream of newspaper headlines proclaiming 'Top state schools may get degree place guarantee'; 'Colleges head-hunt children to fill quotas and win government premiums for inner-city students'; 'The A-levels prodigy no one wants'; 'I won't go to Cambridge now if they pay me'; 'Poor students get easier college entry.' Such articles must have concerned, confused or infuriated students, parents, teachers and academics. There has grown a belief that students may be suffering prejudice against their applications to universities. Sometimes this prejudice is believed to be against students from fee-paying schools; at other times it is thought to be against those from state schools.

Before moving on to see what actually goes on in the selection process it is useful to note that, although 'bias' and 'prejudice' are often used interchangeably, there is a helpful distinction between the two: prejudice implies a pre-formed opinion, especially an unfavourable or irrational one *based on inadequate facts*; bias suggests a leaning or weighting to one side or another, formed (rightly or wrongly) *in the light of the facts*. When Bristol University was boycotted by the independent schools which believed that the university was discriminating against their students (see below), was this a justifiable reaction to an unjustifiable prejudice, or an objection to a bias that was attempting to level the playing field? As Aristotle observed: it is as unfair to treat unequals equally as it is to treat equals unequally.

The basis of student selection

Universities attempt to recruit what they perceive to be the 'best qualified' students for three reasons:

- it is fair and just, and rewards those who have succeeded at school and who have the potential to benefit most from higher education, or are predicted to do so;

- it provides a disappointing but justifiable explanation to those who were not selected – they were not as well qualified;

- 'quality' student entrants and 'able' students gaining success in the final degree exams enhance the university's reputation in league tables and with employers.

The success and fairness of the procedure clearly depend on the definition of 'best qualified', 'potential to benefit most' and 'predicted to benefit most'. The terms can mean different things to different people. To universities such terms have always meant more than assessing people on the basis of A-level grades. How does one distinguish in an A-level grade the academic ability and application of the student from the influence of the school? This is a fundamental problem: the better the school, the more problematic the analysis. There is little point in selecting a student with a glittering array of A levels if he or she does not appear motivated to do the course and appears to have no real interest or potential.

The evaluation of student suitability involves objective criteria (e.g. A-Level grades) with which most people feel comfortable, and subjective criteria, which may be contentious and more difficult to measure. But providing admissions tutors act consistently and in good faith, schools, students and parents have been reassured that the inevitable imperfections in any admissions system apply equally to all candidates. The alarm bells ring when universities appear to discriminate between students on other grounds, or where the basis of their selection is not transparent, whether it has simply not been made clear or whether it has in fact been kept secret. In March 2005, using the Freedom of Information Act, the *Times Higher Education Supplement* obtained confidential advice for admissions tutors showing that the London School of Economics sets aside 40 places a year for pupils from poorly performing schools. The document states that 'These notes should not under any circumstances be discussed with any member of the public, including students, parents and schools.' Clearly, these instructions were of a private nature and favour a number of students from poorly performing schools, presumably state schools. But was this prejudice or a (possibly regretful) response to government pressure? The head of recruitment at LSE responded: 'It's difficult to see this as discrimination given the number of places given to students from independent schools... and 40 places represents just 6 per cent of our home and EU intake.'[1]

Privilege, prejudice and private education

An indication that the media was taking a serious interest in universities discriminating between students became apparent in the 1990s. In 1996 a promising sixth-former Sarah Harness had decided that she wanted to train as a teacher and took pleasure in choosing Reading as her university, visiting on Open Day. She was surprised that the entry requirements for her course seemed so low and she asked for an explanation. An admissions tutor told her curtly that the intention was to avoid alienating those who had not had the privilege of attending 'fee-paying A-level factories'. Ms Harness, who had boarded at The Mount School in North Yorkshire for seven years, became embarrassed and then angry. She nevertheless proceeded with her application, was rejected by Reading University, and studied instead for her degree in English and Education at Canterbury Christ Church College.[2]

A subsequent journalistic investigation revealed that a number of head teachers in the independent sector believed that their pupils were being discriminated against in the race for university places. Dr Jill Clough, headmistress of Wimbledon High School, said one of her girls had applied to a Cambridge college to read mathematics and had been told that higher A-level grades would be required of her because she went to an independent school. 'I feel there should be an equal-opportunity element in selection and background should be irrelevant,' said Dr Clough. 'What I don't like is hidden agendas.' Similarly, Tony Freeman, a teacher with experience in both state and private schools, who was educating his daughters in private schools, described the discreet discrimination in favour of pupils from comprehensive schools as profoundly mistaken. 'Although I pay a fee for my daughters I am buying their schooling for purely educational reasons. I don't think of it as buying some sort of social privilege. I find positive discrimination very troubling,' he said.[3]

Some universities argue that there is a rational basis for such discrimination. A pupil who attains A-grade A levels at an inner-city comprehensive may be more impressive than one with a comparable record from a public school, who has benefited from encouraging parents, small classes, and perhaps private tuition. Some admissions tutors make their preference clear. 'Faced with two pupils of equal ability, one coming from the state system and the other fee-paying, I would choose the state-educated candidate,' said Chris Grosvenor of St Anne's College, Oxford. 'Independent pupils are extremely well coached. If they are unable to achieve more, given the resources available to them, then the less privileged candidates are effectively stronger.'[4] In an article entitled 'Universities shun Eton's high-fliers' in June 1997, Don Carleton, a spokesperson from Bristol University, said: 'If you get three As from Eton, Harrow or Marlborough, you know that they are good schools, with a very stable and well qualified staff. You set that alongside three Bs of a boy in an inner-city comprehensive where there are a lot of pupils to every member of staff, and those three Bs are probably better as an achievement.'[5]

For parents who make substantial sacrifices to send their children to private education, and for the fee-paying schools who educate some 500,000 pupils, such comments make uncomfortable reading. However, care is required in developing a belief on the basis of limited evidence: it is not clear whether such experiences and opinions are isolated instances or reflect something that is regularly happening to half a million pupils. The university or admissions tutor is not invited to present their perspective on what occurred, and it would be invidious for them to comment on an individual student. Also, the views of a particular academic may or may not reflect a generally held belief. Such examples provide little or no idea of the actuality, and will generally only serve to sustain existing beliefs. For, as we examine other evidence, the picture gets more complex.

The view from the other side of the fence

If the pupils from independent schools felt discriminated against, so did those from the state sector. Laura Spence became a cause célèbre in 2000 when Gordon Brown, then chancellor of the exchequer, attacked the selection procedures at Oxford that had rejected Ms Spence, who was a state-school student from Tyneside. The Chancellor's comments were in part factually incorrect and the university was forced to pass public comment on an individual student's performance at interview, an unheard-of debacle.

Evidence that Oxford University was discriminating against *state* pupils was published in the *Oxford Magazine* in 1999 by Professor A.H. Halsey and Dr G. McCrum.[6] The authors analysed the fate of 7,629 pupils who applied to Oxford from state and independent schools between 1994 and 1997. They divided applicants into four groups on the basis of their A-level scores; in each group independent-school pupils were more likely to be offered a place than state-school students. Of the pupils who achieved three A grades, for example, 60 per cent from the independent schools were given a place, as compared to 51 per cent from state schools. Of the students who achieved two As and a B, the figures were 34 and 27 per cent respectively. The article said it was clear that the bias occurred when dons interviewed applicants six months before they took A levels, and the authors argued for the abolition of the interview as a relic from another age.

In an analysis by the educational Sutton Trust, the intake of students was examined at what are purported to be the 13 'top' universities in the country: Cambridge, Oxford, York, Warwick, Bristol, Nottingham, St Andrews, Birmingham, Edinburgh, and Durham, and three London colleges, Imperial, University (UCL) and the LSE. They found that, when grades are the same, public school students are considerably more likely than their state-school counterparts to win places at the 13.[7]

Yet the term 'state school' is itself misleading. The Sutton Trust analysis indicates that more than half of the students coming from 'state schools' actually come from a small group of grammar schools, top academic maintained or church schools. Pupils from an 'average comprehensive' school were reported to have just a 1-in-450 chance of getting a place compared with 1-in-14 for a pupil at an independent school. The philanthropist Peter Lampl, who established the trust, commented: 'I don't think Oxford and Cambridge are at fault. We have an apartheid system of schooling where the vast majority get an inferior education. That is both economically crazy and immoral when we should be giving people opportunities.'[8]

George Walden, a former higher education minister, claimed the problem lay within the schools: 'Why are these figures not better known? Because it is in nobody's interest to confront the truth. The left is embarrassed at the performance of the comprehensives, the right is embarrassed because it is the well heeled who benefit from the comprehensives' failure, and Oxbridge is embarrassed by the lack of social mix.'[9]

Professor Valentine Cunningham, senior English tutor at Corpus Christi College, Oxford, also reacted strongly against ministers' attacks on Oxford's alleged 'elitist bias'. In a detailed article he wrote:

> Oxford University is being most unfairly vilified for its admissions practices. The attackers, silly and stupid, have selected the wrong target for whatever legitimate social anger they claim as motivation. Many applicants at Oxford are disappointed – and from every kind of school... But these disappointments are not organised or systematic. We do not discriminate by age or gender, class, ethnicity, region or type of school, as our detractors profess to think... Still, there is huge disproportion of private-sector students at Oxford compared with the national percentage of state-school pupils. No other topic so preoccupies Oxford common rooms.[10]

In December 2004 research carried out by Oxford University, 'Social Factors in Admissions to the University of Oxford', analysed the applications of 4,539 candidates to 11 colleges, focusing on GCSE scores. The aim was to establish if candidates from different backgrounds, independent schools or state schools, have the same chance of being offered a place. It was concluded that sixth formers from private schools have less chance of gaining a conditional offer than state-school pupils with the same academic record. This difference remained when AS results and predicted A-level results were taken into account.

One possible explanation given in the report is that 'Admission tutors might be "discounting" the grades of independent school pupils because they believe that teaching at these schools improves the grades of their students but without lasting improvements in their academic performance.' But what was the degree of difference between the two groups? Professor Heath, author of the report, emphasised that 'we are talking about marginal differences between very good and very, very good candidates. In simple terms, if you give 100 places to candidates through conditional offers you would have to take three places from state schools and give them to independent school pupils to give equal chances at the margin.'[11]

The many efforts of Oxford and Cambridge to broaden their social intake have certainly been ineffective. Obtaining data under the Freedom of Information laws, the *Sunday Times* provided a league table of the state schools most successful at getting pupils into Oxford and Cambridge universities in 2006. The majority of successful applicants came from fewer than 20 per cent of the state secondary schools; most were from grammar schools or sixth-form colleges.

	Cambridge	Oxford
students from state schools	48%	47%
students from independent schools	38%	43%
students from overseas or other sources	14%	10%

A total of 69 schools out of 3,400 were identified as providing at least five pupils who had started at Cambridge. The figures showed 118 schools with four or more offers of places at Oxford, with 16 schools having 10 or more offers.[12]

The totality of the above evidence therefore indicates that concerns of discrimination against the public schools were largely unfounded. Indeed, there was an emerging theme that it was the state-school and not private-school pupils who were disadvantaged. However, concerns about the consideration given to factors other than academic ability or potential raised an entirely new development in selection procedures with the potential for discrimination. The issue has caused heated discussion and accusations of social engineering. It is one of the most controversial issues in secondary and higher education and within our society.

The Government intervenes

In October 2002 the higher education minister, Margaret Hodge, said: 'Under the current administration's procedures, there is, if anything, discrimination against bright, young, high-achieving people from state schools... The Russell Group are not admitting a fair proportion of high-achieving kids from state schools.'[13]

On 8 April 2003, in an article in *The Times* entitled 'Universities "must show they are open to all"', the secretary of state for higher education and skills, Charles Clarke, was quoted as saying that elite universities must abandon their socially exclusive image if they want to convince the Government's new access regulator that they should be allowed to increase tuition fees: 'I think Oxford and Cambridge should specifically be looking to a modern image of themselves, applying to the best and most talented people irrespective of social class. To that extent, the *Brideshead Revisited* image which Oxbridge sometimes transmits isn't appropriate for that modern age. It's 75 years out of date.'[14]

Universities, he said, in deciding on offers, would be expected to consider social class, the average levels of achievement at the pupils' schools, and whether their parents are graduates. This was a political development of major magnitude with profound implications. Universities were to be driven down the road of widening access. It was something Bristol University had been doing for several years, attracting vitriolic attacks and a boycott by most independent schools.

The Bristol experience

The University of Bristol was one of the first universities to recruit potential high achievers held back by their underprivileged educational background. The development was modelled on the success of a scheme operated by the university's law department since 1993, designed to take in 'promising applications from schools with poor A-level records'.

Whilst Oxford and Cambridge have tried to attract more students from comprehensive schools, Bristol's initiative was regarded by many as the first to show positive discrimination. Sir John Kingman, the then vice-chancellor of Bristol, described the strategy for widening the pool from which it draws its students as 'the most important paper for a decade' to come before the university council. Mr Vivian Anthony, Secretary of the Headmasters' and Headmistresses' Conference, which represents the leading independent schools, said he was horrified by the scheme and predicted a legal challenge: 'There must be a serious possibility of a parent, whose child had higher grades than others being admitted, testing whether the university was breaking the law. We would not be backward in supporting them.'[15] Bristol stuck to its guns and was boycotted.

The procedure at Bristol, referred to then as the Alternative Admissions Scheme and now as the Widening Participation

Strategy, takes applications that, on the normal criteria applied when candidates are first considered, do not merit a conditional offer of a place and submits them to scrutiny again by a second panel. Applicants who attend schools or colleges with poor A-level records may be made lower offers. Up to ten per cent of the places have been allocated in this way.

Since 1999 all Bristol's faculties have been expected to 'examine applications in a wider context'. Don Carleton, the university's spokesman, said: 'We want to broaden the social spectrum to pick up on talent we might have been missing. Good, but not outstanding A levels, achieved in an educationally deprived setting, often show the commitment and self-motivation that makes for success at university… The offer will still be very challenging in the circumstances in which they find themselves. They are not second class students: we are taking account of the education-ally disadvantaged context of their application and assessing their potential.'[16]

At a meeting with admissions tutors from Bristol University and the LSE, representatives of independent schools demanded to know why tutors were turning away large numbers of their pupils in favour of state-school children with poorer qualifications. It was believed that arbitrary decisions were being made to exclude privately educated children; both institutions had recently introduced measures to widen access. Eric Thomas, the vice-chancellor of Bristol, explained that because a degree from Bristol conferred real personal advantages the university had a moral obligation to widen access:

> We do not indulge in social engineering. Our goal is to take the individuals with the most potential and make them fly. Such a potential is not measured only by predicted A-level grades. We have objective evidence that students from schools whose average A-level score is three Cs or lower do better in their degrees than their direct equivalents from schools whose A-level average exceeds that.[17]

Figures released from the Higher Education Funding Council for England in December 2002 showed that the LSE's state-school intake had increased from 58 to 66 per cent in a year, while Bristol had raised its figure from 57 to 60 per cent. This had been achieved at Bristol by weighting grades of applicants according to the average achievement of their school, a system that is subtle enough to distinguish between different levels of independent schools as well as between state and private institutions. By this measure, a B at a comprehensive is rated the same as an A at a good private school.

The Headmasters' and Headmistresses' Conference and the Girls' Schools Association acknowledged that universities faced a difficult task in differentiating between highly qualified candidates for places on oversubscribed courses:

> But we do not believe there is evidence or justification
> for the making of differential offers to candidates merely
> on the ground of average school performance based on
> raw examination results. Information about a student's
> background (social class, schooling, parental education,
> and income) should not be available to those making
> the selection but be recorded separately for national
> monitoring.[18]

The attempt to remove bias in selection put the two organisations, representing 450 leading schools, in direct opposition to the Government on admissions.

Many letters to the press or articles railed against this method of 'widening access'. The chairman of the Campaign for Real Education, a parents' pressure group, criticised the new policies as discriminatory: 'While we may want to see more disadvantaged students in higher education, this is social engineering of the worst kind. Our great universities are going to become local institutions at this rate.'[19] Stephen Glover wrote: 'It is a monstrous injustice. I am amazed that dons, whom you would expect to believe in equity and academic excellence, can have involved themselves in such a shabby and dishonest exercise.'[20]

Do academics believe that they have behaved in a shabby and dishonest way? In an article entitled 'We dons are being asked to destroy what we hold most dear', John Adamson, a fellow of Peterhouse who helps select candidates for Cambridge University, described himself as having become a partner in fraud. In respect to the Government's demands, however, he noted that the financial penalties for non-compliance would ensure obedience:

> We dons will be faced with a choice: either to accept the government's cash and conditions, agreeing to quotas by social background and abandoning the principle of selection on merit, or we stick to meritocracy and commit financial suicide by forgoing the right to charge fees... there is little doubt that the universities will dance to the government's tune.
>
> The irony of these new arrangements is that they will not only hurt the independent schools, which currently win a disproportionate number of the A-level places; they will penalise successful state schools as well. Able state-sector candidates with three A-grades seem certain to be among those pushed aside as universities make way for their cash-producing quota of dullards...
>
> This is not to deny that there is an embarrassing, even shameful imbalance between the success rates of State v Independent candidates. Any education system in which the state controls more than 90 per cent of the schools, and yet manages to win barely half the available Oxford and Cambridge places, is obviously letting a lot of potential talent go unrealised.[21]

No one has accused the universities that have some 90 per cent of all their places being filled with students from state schools of prejudicing or biasing their intake towards pupils from the state system! These were the students who applied and were accepted.

An over-abundance of qualified applicants

The academic community faces a daunting task in attempting to select the best qualified students with the greatest potential. As Graham Able, headmaster of Dulwich College and chairman of the Headmasters' and Headmistresses' Conference, has observed: 'There is no evidence of Oxford being biased. What the research does show is the impossibly difficult task admission tutors have when faced with the same grades and predicted grades.'[22]

As a result, many are now considering methods of selection that would have been thought preposterous only a few years ago. The traditional selection process was based on the applicant gaining suitable grades in the A-level examination. This worked satisfactorily for universities and subjects that were not heavily over-prescribed: students with the best grades were awarded a place. The process appeared fair and defensible and was not contentious. As we have seen, however, it has been compromised by the fact that the Government's requirement to widen participation and broaden selection criteria has moved the goalposts. In addition, some subject areas, such as medicine or English, are heavily oversubscribed and there has been a concomitant increase in the number of students with top A-level grades, which in turn have been hotly disputed as grade inflation. John Witheridge, headmaster of Charterhouse, notes:

> Back in 1996, Charterhouse scored 38 per cent A grades (70 per cent this year) and 68 per cent A and B grades (91 per cent in 2007). If only my staff and I could take all the credit for such a striking improvement during my 11 years as headmaster. Alas, we all know the sobering truth about grade inflation. This year's overall results are up for the 25th successive year. The proportion of A grades nationally now exceeds 25 per cent and the pass rate is 97 per cent. What kind of examination is this?[23]

These factors ensure that, for many students, A-level grades are now the key to open only the first door to access the university system. The key to the second door was identified by Margaret Hodge when minister for lifelong learning and higher education: 'They [individual universities] should select applicants by merit, based on their potential to succeed. We encourage universities to use a wide range of measures to assess that potential.'[24] Using past achievements to predict future potential is problematic in its own right. But to attempt to measure the 'potential to succeed' will require fascinating and creative solutions.

Is the 'potential to succeed' related to prior schooling?

Earlier in this chapter Chris Grosvenor of St Anne's College, Oxford, was quoted as saying that, all other things being equal, the state-educated pupil would be considered a stronger candidate than one from an independent school, having 'succeeded despite the odds'. If this is the case – and others have expressed a similar view – it would provide a powerful reason for carefully assessing the educational outcomes from state and independent schools.

There is evidence that the teaching afforded by independent schools confers a substantial advantage in terms of A-level output. This was shown in 1994 in a detailed study undertaken by the Department of Education involving 157,000 pupils, comparing the performance of six different types of school. The aim of the study was to measure the 'value added' by the different types of schools to the examination performance of their pupils. This was achieved by analysing the performance of all 157,000 candidates who the previous year had taken two or more A or AS levels (excluding general studies) in relation to what the same pupils had achieved two years previously at GCSE.[25]

Table 3.1

Points scored at GCSE	Percentage of pupils in secondary education in different types of school gaining 20+ points at A-level					
	Independent	*Grammar (old)*	*Grammar (LEA)*	*Sixth-Form college*	*Comprehensive*	*Further Education college*
Under 35	24	8	5	5	2	4
35–39	20	3	6	4	2	4
40–44	25	8	8	7	5	8
45–49	39	12	14	17	12	15
50–54	49	29	31	31	27	27
55–59	67	49	53	61	45	45
60–64	84	73	80	70	71	65
65–69	83	67	75	77	73	69
70 plus	94	73	89	83	87	85

Scoring: A-Level A grade = 10 points, B = 8, etc. GCSE A = 7, B = 6, G = 1

Source: Department of Education

The most striking feature is the superiority of independent-school candidates over their peers at every measured band of ability. Also, the groups showing the most dramatic success are those with 'modest ability' in sixth-form terms, those who scored 35 to 49 points at GCSE, with the improvements gradually and necessarily decreasing as the baseline GCSE attainments increased.

This success surprised even the independent schools themselves, since they considered that they had already added considerable value to pupils by the time they took GCSE, which makes it harder to improve further at A level. The reasons for the success were not clear. Possibly small classes, supervised private study, and greater non-classroom contact with teachers for boarding students may have contributed to the results obtained.

A crucial factor, however, according to heads of wide-ability schools, is that exam success can be almost self-perpetuating if the right culture is established. David Exham of Bloxam in Oxfordshire said: 'A lot of academic success comes from pupils being confident. If they can see that their predecessors did well, and go into a course assuming they will do the same, they probably will.'[26] He believed that expectations and motivations are buttressed by the fees. Parents, looking for a return, try to provide a supportive home environment, while pupils become more conscious of the money spent on their behalf.

Other heads talk of comprehensives and sixth-form colleges that handle A-stream pupils very well, but challenge them on performance with the B-stream. According to the general secretary of the Independent Schools' Bursars Association, Mr Mike Sant, 'The biggest difference between independent schools and maintained schools is the pupil – teacher ratio, and that's a huge cost. We have seven per cent of pupils but we have 14 per cent of teachers (7.7 pupils per teacher as compared with 17-to-one in state secondaries). Of course, that's what parents are paying for.'[27]

The complexity of this study means it is unlikely to be repeated but, if it were, the results today might well show independent schools doing even better. In any event, the figures certainly provide a new context for the simple league s of student ability as measured in A-level performance: the type of school can dramatically affect a pupil's A-level performance, given the same initial level of academic ability.

The independent schools are caught on the horns of a dilemma. The quality of their instruction can greatly enhance a pupil's ability to pass examinations – which impresses parents – but these impressive results support the belief of universities and government that an important component of their pupils' success in A-level examinations is a reflection of their well supported school. The *inherent ability* of the student and his or her future potential remain uncertain.

It is the Government's contention that able students with *potential* for higher education are to be found in schools outside the independent sector, possibly with lower A-level grades; and that they can be attracted to realise this potential by broadening access, taking into consideration other factors believed to reflect motivation and potential academic strength. If this is correct, the performance of state school pupils at university – a demonstration of that potential – should equal that of students educated in the independent sector. Is there evidence of such performance?

Emerging effects of widening participation

In December 2002 Robin Naylor and Jeremy Smith, two Warwick University researchers, examined the results of 42,281 full-time graduates leaving university in 1993. They concluded that the chance of a private-school student obtaining a 'good' degree' was between 5.4 and 6.5 percentage points lower than that of a state-school student with the same A levels. They suggested that the reason for this disparity was that better coaching, which private-school students received, camouflaged their lower natural ability. Furthermore, Dr Smith said: 'We found that the independent school students who were the least successful went to the highest fee-paying school.'[28] In response to this last observation, Dick Davidson of the Independent Schools Council, said it was silly to relate fee scales to degree performance because cheaper day schools were often highly selective. 'It's a bit of a cheap shot,' he said. 'I think that the universities are rather less keen to accept that pupils find the teaching in many universities to be poorer than that which they enjoyed at school.'[29]

In January 2003 interim results from analysts at the Higher Education Funding Council for England (HEFCE) were reported at a conference on widening access to higher education. Bahram Bekhradnia, director of policy at HEFCE when the study began, said that a better education and a better preparation for exams could explain the effect. However, he also said: 'Pupils from independent schools with a given score at A level performed significantly less well at university than their state-school peers. Institutions may well be justified in making more demanding offers to candidates from independent schools, who will on average perform less well than their state-school peers with equivalent A-level grades.' The difference was equivalent to two A-level grades.[30]

In the Partners scheme in Newcastle, local teachers have helped to identify pupils who could benefit from degree courses. The students received lower offers, but were given a chance to prove their abilities at a summer school after A levels. Newcastle University was typically offering three grade Cs at A level, instead of a normal course requirement of three Bs, to selected students from 56 partner schools and colleges in the north-east. It had no lack of applicants and the Partners scheme spread to almost all subjects at the university, including dentistry and medicine. Newcastle medical school took its first intake of 10 Partners students in 2002 and said that, eight weeks after they began, they performed better than average in all three areas assessed by their first progress test: skills, knowledge and understanding, and personal and professional development.[31] An account of the current Partners scheme at Newcastle University is found at www.ncl.ac.uk/partners.

These findings, along with Bristol's experience which we looked at earlier, raise two questions:

- Are A-level grades a reliable marker of future academic potential at university?

- Why do pupils from state schools appear to achieve better results at university?

The results appear to offer evidence to support the long-held suspicions of admissions tutors. Some pupils brought up within the sometimes rugged challenges of the state-school system may be better prepared for the rough and ready realities of a state-sponsored university education. It may also raise questions as to the comparative values of being educated in the independent or state system.

But the present evidence is partly anecdotal. With such important implications for students, parents, schools and universities, it is imperative that universities publish their findings on this subject as they would any other research. Indeed, given the extreme sensitivity of the issues involved, it is to be regretted that this has not already occurred. It is also just as important to establish whether the results achieved at Newcastle and Bristol universities are observed at other universities. If so, it may provide a defining moment in attempting to re-establish a more reliable mechanism for the transition between secondary and higher education.

Bias by students

There remains one final factor to consider in bias or prejudice in student intake, one which is often ignored: that imposed by students on themselves. Bias, or even prejudice, can take many forms, and perceptions and preconceptions in the minds of school teachers, parents and other advisers, which are picked up by the students themselves, become reflected in the biases that appear in the actual student figures. It may be questioned why, out of all the universities in the country, a significant number of state-school pupils appear to avoid making applications to Oxbridge and the Russell Group of universities.

The lack of success in attracting state-school pupils may reflect an anti-Oxbridge climate among state-school teachers. 'It goes against the grain to select out their pupils for elite universities, whereas in most selective and independent schools their status depends on the Oxbridge count,' said one retired grammar-school head. David Adelman, principal of Godalming College in Surrey, said it wasn't always in pupils' interests to push them for Oxbridge: 'For those that don't get offered a place it can be demoralising and put them off striving to get into other universities.'[32]

Prejudice in applications can also appear at the other end of the spectrum: the 'Oxbridge, then the rest' attitude. Professor Eric Thomas, the vice-chancellor of Bristol, writing also as a parent, raised this further issue regarding the success or failure of students in applying to universities:

> It is a grave error for them to believe that other universities merely exist as a convenient repository for students who have not gained entry to Oxbridge... Some personal statements [on UCAS forms] are entirely focused on the course being applied to at Oxbridge, with scant attention paid to why they are applying to the other universities... Why should they offer a place to someone who makes no mention of the special characteristics of their course when they literally have hundreds of applicants who do?[33]

Imbalances have also been identified with regard to individual courses. Those published by the *Times Higher Education Supplement* in April 2004 showed a breakdown of students who applied for full-time university places through UCAS.[34]

Table 3.2 Admissions by social class

Subject group	Higher social class %	Lower social class %	Unidentified social class
Medicine and dentistry	74	14	13
Modern languages, literature and related	68	20	11
History and philosophical studies	67	20	14
Linguistics, classics and related	64	21	15
Physical sciences	63	24	14
Combined subjects	59	24	17
Law	58	24	19
Biological sciences	57	26	17
Social studies	57	23	20
Architecture, building and planning	54	25	20
Mass communications and documentation	53	26	21
Subjects allied to medicine	52	27	22
Engineering and technologies	51	26	22
Veterinary science, agriculture and related	50	30	20
Education	49	31	19
Business and administrative studies	49	27	24
No preferred subject group	49	24	27
Creative arts and design	47	28	25
Mathematical and computer sciences	46	27	27

(Students were identified by UCAS as belonging to one of seven social classes, which the newspaper grouped as 'higher' (classes 1, 2 and 3, accounting for 37 per cent of the population) and 'lower' (classes 4, 5, 6 and 7, accounting for 35 per cent of the population); the remainder were the non-working or unemployed, students or otherwise unclassified.)

Source: *Times Higher Education Supplement*

The breakdown clearly shows that students from poor backgrounds stand much less chance of securing a degree place than those from more prosperous backgrounds when applying for medicine and certain other subject groups.

Do the substantial differences occur at the point of application or selection, or more likely both?

In the most detailed study ever undertaken in the UK, HEFCE research published in 2005 suggests that 34 per cent of students from 'low-participation areas' (areas or regions which traditionally have a low proportion of students entering higher education) lived at home while they studied, while only 15 per cent of students from 'high participation areas' did the same. Why does a geographical location influence the choice of where to study for so many students from low-participation areas in a way it does not for students from more affluent areas? Penny Burke, lecturer in higher education in the School of Educational Foundations and Policy Studies at the Institute of Education, University of London, says the choices made by students from poor neighbourhoods are not simply a matter of money or practical problems such as travel or accommodation. She says:

> For example, work by Diane Reay and colleagues highlights that making choices about where to study is not only about material and practical issues – it is also about deeper cultural issues… They tend not to choose more prestigious universities where they risk 'not fitting in' and being a minority and where they would have to travel to unfamiliar areas outside of their local communities… Complex issues in relation to practical and material issues, age, ability, class, gender, family and identity all shape decisions about where to study.[35]

The same HEFCE study also found 'modest' differences in the choices of course that students from 'low-participation areas' made compared with teenagers from more affluent areas, for example:

Table 3.3

	'high participation'	'low participation'
Languages, medicine, humanities, agriculture	18%	11%
Mathematics, computer science, nursing, education	16%	21%

Source: HEFCE

A poll, carried out by ExamAid and the Association of Colleges (AoC), of 2,700 students aged 15 to 19 years, who were mostly in further education colleges, revealed that many believed that they had made the wrong choice of GCSEs or A levels. Only a third believed that their courses would definitely help them to achieve their career ambitions. Judith Norrington, the AoC's director of curriculum and quality said that students needed access to better advice when choosing their AS and A-level subjects. The survey showed that 80 per cent of students had taken their decision on their own.[36] So students, especially those who do not turn to reliable sources of advice, may be restricting their own choice before they even reach the sixth form.

A different sort of bias was termed a 'hidden scandal' by John Dunford, general secretary of the Secondary Heads Association (now the Association of School and College Leaders). He sees students rejecting sciences and modern languages A levels because it is perceived to be harder to get top grades in those subjects:

> The rise in interest in psychology is a consequence of what people are perceiving, that maths and physics are harder and they can get better grades in psychology... It is incredibly worrying. Maths, sciences and foreign languages are subjects that the country needs and it is totally bizarre that they are the hardest A levels... We are producing a nation of psychologists when the country desperately needs more highly qualified scientists and linguists... The Tomlinson inquiry should be making exams in all subjects of comparable standard and that is not the case at the moment... Since most university courses don't discriminate between grades in different subjects, head teachers are bound to advise students to take subjects in which they can achieve best grades.

These views were rejected by the Minister for School Standards and the chief executive of the Qualifications Curriculum Authority.[37]

Ultimately, the choice of university and subject will always remain a matter of personal preference and obtaining sui A-level grades to gain admission. But for a child with foresight who wishes to maximise his or her chances of entering higher education, based on the most recent HEFCE findings, the following guidance, with tongue in cheek, could be recommended:

- be born a girl (girls at university now outnumber boys);
- take care to be born in September (if every child had the same chance as those born in September there would be an extra 12,000 undergraduates each year);
- be born to parents who live in a 'high-participation' or middle-class area!

Final reflections

This particular journey into the world of potential bias and prejudice in the selection of students has revealed deep concerns by the universities and academic staff, schools and their pupils, their parents and the Government. There are at present few winners in a tale of good intentions merging imperceptibly into self-interest, of universities not being fully transparent in their findings, and all compounded by the law of unintended consequences.

There is little evidence that universities have been *prejudiced* in their selection of students. On the subject of *bias*, however, the so-called premier league of UK universities is perceived to have contributed to a culture, established over decades, where a disproportionate number of their students came from independent schools and were of middle-class background. But this was not necessarily solely the result of bias in selection. A significant and disproportionate number of state-school pupils did not even apply to these universities: one cannot be biased against pupils who do not apply, although even then universities must take some responsibility for their historical image which may be off-putting. But, universities have now been given targets to improve the number of state-school students in those universities where their number is considered by government to be too low.

So will higher education have to look forward to increasing quotas of dullards and a loss of potential talent? Will the discrimination apply to students from both independent and highly successful state schools and treat them all as of 'independent status'. It would appear bizarre that state schools, having risen to the Government's challenge to improve their performance to that of the independent sector, may be penalised for having done so.

In May 2007, however, there was an even more unexpected outcome to a decade of emphasis by the Blair government on equality in education. It was reported that parents were turning to private schooling, the numbers rising from

505,450 in 2006 to 509,093 in 2007. The greatest changes were for sixth formers, up 1.5 per cent from 79,753 to 80,958. The independent school head teachers believed that the prime minister's policies were responsible, with more parents being made aware of the importance of trained teachers to teach maths and science, the importance of compulsory language instruction, and better student–staff ratios. Additional factors may reflect that some parents are better off financially and are prioritising their children's education.[38]

In any event, figures in July 2007 from the Higher Education Statistics Agency showed only slow or inconsistent progress in raising the number of students from state schools and disadvantaged backgrounds. Figures for under-21s in full-time undergraduate degree courses in Britain 2005–06 showed a rise in entrants from state schools over a four-year period of 0.33 per cent per year, up to 87.4 per cent. In England only 29.1 per cent of young people from low socio-economic groups started courses, up 0.3 per cent a year. Comparable figures for Wales, Scotland and Northern Ireland all showed falls to previous values.

The Russell Group was an inevitable focus of interest. The latest figures show that the University of Oxford, at 53.7 per cent of new undergraduates coming from state schools (benchmark 75.4 per cent), is holding steady. The University of Sheffield, another Russell Group member, increased its state-school pupil entrants to 83.8 per cent (benchmark 79.7 per cent). It may be relevant to note that the performance indicators date from the year before the £3,000 top-up tuition fees were introduced in England. The National Union of Students said that 'dramatic improvement' was needed, but nevertheless Bill Rammell, the higher education minister for England, said universities were 'on the right track'.[39]

Universities are investigating a number of initiatives in an attempt to improve the selection process. These include:

- asking A-level applicants for a breakdown of their marks;

- improved interviews;

- supplementary entrance tests such as the American style Scholastic Aptitude Tests (SATs);

- the Biomedical Admissions Test (Bmat) (which consists of a 60-minute test of aptitude and skills, a 30-minute test of scientific knowledge, and a 30-minute writing test);

- the introduction of a lottery system;
- the introduction of the National Admissions Test for Law, which is designed, like so many other tests, to 'provide objective evaluations of candidates from a wide range of social and educational backgrounds by assessing general intellectual skills of comprehension, analysis, logic and judgement'.

There remains uncertainty within the academic community as to the validity and ethics of selection criteria. A sense of social and educational fair play is balanced against the possibility of discrimination and social engineering. Controversially, the Government has driven universities to broaden the scope of their selection criteria to include the nature of the pupil's school and the average A-level grade of the school, parental background and other factors that a university may wish to acknowledge as predictors of future student potential.

In broadening access to pupils from state schools who do not necessarily have the same (or as high) A-level grades, but do have other factors reflecting motivation and potential academic strength, it is of great interest that these students have been found to perform at least as well as their peers at university. Indeed, there is evidence that they may have achieved better performance and degrees than their peers. Such evidence cannot be ignored.

Chapter 4

The League Tables Minefield

The League Tables Minefield

LEAGUE TABLES HAVE become a national obsession. For many years there have been good food guides, good pub guides and, more recently and more seriously, even a good euthanasia guide. But now prisons and police forces, schools and hospitals and numerous other categories of organisation have become subject to assessment and ranking in an attempt to distinguish the lustrous from the lacklustre. In particular, the Government has attempted to create a culture of accountability and efficiency in the public services by defining and measuring standards from which they can establish and then publicise league tables.

However, the usefulness and reliability of such league tables has been frequently called into question. With respect to hospital rankings, the reaction of James Johnson, chairman of the British Medical Association, to the introduction of star ratings was:

> I don't think any doctors would judge how well a hospital is doing by looking at star ratings... [they are a] fairly useless publication which only measure how good a hospital is at meeting political targets. They do not mean anything clinically and patients should be made aware of that.[1]

When it was announced in 2005 that, for the first time, the best state schools had overtaken their fee-paying rivals in league tables, the Independent Schools Council accused the Government of rendering performance tables meaningless by taking into account hundreds of extra qualifications: 'They no longer have any value whatever in reporting on meaningful achievement in key academic subjects or serious vocational subjects.'[2] Could the same comments apply to university league tables?

The order of appearance in a league table can be likened to the cast list in the credits for a play. Indeed, both reflect degrees of theatre. However, there are clear differences between the response to a production created by an academic or hospital league table and the curtain call of a stage performance. First, the ones who are first to receive the accolade of a theatre audience are the vital and enthusiastic support staff, without which there would be no show;

last to appear are the 'stars'. Secondly, all actors in a theatre are warmly applauded and encouraged; there are no negative or punitive connotations taken against the order of appearance. Thirdly, all staff and players, no matter how modest or distinguished, work closely together to ensure the finest and most pleasing outcome for all concerned, a marked contrast with the often dramatic but destructive power of a league table.

A crucial feature of a league table is that there are perceived to be losers as well as winners, with self-righteous indignation or disdain for the 'lower ranks'. Also in an attempt to hide the inevitable and embarrassingly fine gradation of differences between the contestants of most league tables, where comparative numerical values merge imperceptibly from one contestant into the next, league tables frequently require subjective, artificial and nonsensical demarcations. The illusory power of these distinctions is quite remarkable and will fool most of the people most of the time, including some of the contestants!

Most people, and certainly all parents and students, will be aware of the very fine lines that distinguish one grade of school examination from another. Each summer, when GCSE and A-level results are announced, there are accusations of subjective marking, cries for regrading and laments of 'I was only two points off an A.' The compilation of university league tables is even more open to inconsistencies, anomalies and misdirection.

To the organisations and individuals affected by any questionable rankings, the consequences are not humorous and indeed can be very serious, with a potential loss of prestige and morale, influence and resources. With this in mind it is not surprising that all institutions arrange their submissions in the most favourable light; all play games. And some have been shown to cheat.

League tables and rankings of academic institutions and their activities are probably no worse than those in other areas, which means to say that they can be very bad. But are university league tables 'educationally meaningless' in the way that some hospital rankings are 'clinically meaningless'?

What a typical league table tells us

When *The Times* published Britain's first University League Table in October 1992 it reported 'a withering statement' from the Committee of Vice-Chancellors and Principals of the Universities of the United Kingdom (now Universities UK): 'We believe the tables are wrong in principle, flawed in execution and constructed upon data which are not uniform, are ill-defined, and in places demonstrably false.'[3] Although some indicators used to rank universities have improved, most academics still retain a dislike for league tables or for comparing one university with another. The presidents of 30 schools in the US have pledged not to use the rankings to promote their institutions and are urging 600 of their counterparts to join them.[4] Others are parodying the rankings. Jonathan Gottshall, a former university student, ranks universities in the USA and Canada based on the health and population of campus squirrels: 'The quality of an institution can often be determined by the size, health and behaviour of the squirrel population on campus,' said Mr Gottshall, who employs a five-squirrel scale.[5] Then there is the fictitious College Ranking Service, which echoes a criticism that other league tables reflect the wealth of universities more than any other measure. The College Ranking Service Annual Announcement on 17 August 2007 reported that for the seventh straight year:

- The CRS has found that prestige in colleges and universities correlates with the size of the endowment. The richest schools are the most prestigious.
- Harvard, Yale, Princeton... are all incredibly prestigious and wealthy. In fact they are so wealthy that the CRS wonders why anyone continues to donate money to them. They don't need your money, folks. They have billions and billions of dollars. By continuing to solicit money from you, they are just being greedy.
- The CRS has found no correlation between the prestige of a university and the quality of its education.
- The CRS found that state universities continue to be squeezed by state governments... But they are the engines that provide this country with its educated workforce. Without Harvard et al., this country would still do well. Without UCLA et al., this country would be in real trouble (www.rankyourcollege.com).

Sixteen years after the critical comments of the Vice-Chancellors and Principals, it was finally admitted in June 2007 that rankings may exert a corruptive influence.[6]

But will we cease to publish university league tables? An editorial in the *Times Higher Education Supplement* in June 2007 concluded that they would remain: 'For all their faults, league tables allow institutions, those who work in them and those who wish to attend them to be compared and evaluated. They exist because people want them.'[7] This view is reinforced by surveys carried out by universities and others showing that:

- up to 80 per cent of university applicants consult the league tables published annually in quality newspapers;

- while disapproving of league tables, the majority of universities and departments are only too pleased to acknowledge their successes if appearing in the upper echelons! Only London Metropolitan University was excluded from the *Sunday Times* league table guide in 2006 after witholding data from the newspaper.

Such league tables are generally a well intentioned attempt to help prospective students choose an appropriate university. They provide a relatively simple solution to a complex problem, and as such have some merit. But for academic staff, teachers and parents who are advising prospective students, their limitations cannot be ignored. It takes a canny reader with some insider knowledge to read between the lines.

Let us do some analysis on a typical example: *The Times* University League Table for 2007. It is the measurements or ratings that are used to compare universities that are the crucial factors as to whether the ranking has credibility or meaning. Precisely the same comments would apply to the compilation of any other league table.

The Times University League Table 2007

The full league table covers 109 universities; below, for our present purposes, is an extract covering just three.

Table 4.1

The Times *Good University Guide 2007: Top Universities 2007 League Table* (http://www.timesonline.co.uk/displayPopup/0,102571,00.html)										
Ranking and institution	Student satisfaction	Research assessment	Entry standards	Student–staff ratio	Library and computing	Facilities spend	Good honours	Graduate prospects	Completion	Total
1. Oxford	–	6.5	511.7	13	1656	364	88.4	74.8	97.7	1000
30. Essex	15.2	5.6	308.7	14.6	643	307	55.4	62.8	85.7	677
60. Nottingham Trent	14.6	2.8	275.9	20.5*	611	145*	55.8	63.4	84.1	497

* Institution provided its own data.

The nine key aspects that contribute to the table rankings are weighted 1.5 for satisfaction and research and 1.0 for the rest, and finally summed to give a total score for the university. If a university was missing any data, the total score was based on the remaining data available. The individual scores were then transformed to a scale where the top score was set at 1000 and the remainder as a proportion of the top score. What exactly are the measurements and are they meaningful? Below are the qualifying explanations for each aspect and a closer look at what these actually mean.

Student satisfaction

Taken from part of the annual National Student Survey (NSS). The survey is a measure of student opinion, not a direct measure of quality.

The NSS in 2005 was the first authoritative assessment of university student opinion in the UK. Whilst weighted equally to research, it provides the first and most relevant expression of the student experience, from the students' own daily experience. The data is missing for Oxford, Cambridge and Warwick, which boycotted the survey. Since 'the total score was based on the remaining data available', other universities might feel that these universities are unfairly advantaged. If the NSS is being used it should be applied to all. Furthermore, it is extraordinary for the league table to disparage the views of 157,000 undergraduate students as 'not a direct measure of quality'. It would be interesting to hear the response of the students. Perhaps more revealing, why was it necessary to make the comment? The NSS is discussed in more detail later in this chapter.

Research assessment

Average quality of research by all staff at the university, from the 2001 Research Assessment Exercise.

The purported standard of research conducted in a UK university is probably the single most important factor in whether it is recognised as a 'top', 'elite', 'prestige', 'premier', 'best', 'first division' university, by the university itself and both nationally and internationally. Research prestige creates a powerful 'halo effect' which affects the perceived quality of all the activities of the university, including teaching. For an undergraduate, however, the research activities of a university are not necessarily the best indicator of teaching excellence. Chapter 5 explores this misconception in more detail.

Entry standards

Average UCAS tariff score of new students under age 21, from the Higher Education Statistics Agency (HESA) in 2003–04.

The UCAS tariff is based on a scoring system in which, at A level, an A grade is 120 points, B 100, C 80, D 60, and E 40. AS grades are worth half as much. This figure is a reasonable measure of the academic ability of the undergraduate student cohort at an institution, although there is at present no satisfactory way of scoring other entrance qualifications, such as the International Baccalaureate. It says nothing about the quality of provision for aspiring students, although it may give an indication of a student's peer group.

Student–staff ratio

Average number of students per staff member at the university, taken from HESA data for 2003–04.

The student–staff ratio (SSR) is a convenient, and the most widely used, means of expressing the number of academic staff available to undertake teaching duties. External accreditation or professional bodies are very particular about SSRs. Their influence to maintain appropriate SSRs is one of the key ways of ensuring that universities honour their obligations to support individual courses properly. Most academic staff would consider it fundamental that students require not merely professionally trained staff, but *sufficient* staff to teach the increasing number of students. There are two points to note. First, the league table figure is the average *for all departments within a university;* it does not describe the ratio for a particular department or school. Ratios will vary enormously between different types of departments. For example, dental students about to attempt their first filling or tooth extraction may, reassuringly, obtain an SSR of one! To establish a *meaningful* SSR, potential students need to know the ratio for a particular department, which cannot be determined from the table.

Secondly, SSRs may be determined on the basis of *all* full-time staff within a department, but this may include research-only staff. The 2005–06 figures showed that about a quarter of academic staff were research-only and did not undertake any teaching. About a quarter were teaching-only and roughly half the staff divide their time between teaching and research. It is not clear from an SSR what proportion of time 'teaching and research' staff spend on teaching (see Chapter 6).

Library and computing spend

> *Average expenditure per student on library and computing facilities, from HESA data between 2001 and 2004.*

This is the expenditure per full-time-equivalent student on books, journals, computer software and hardware and staff, factors directly related to the provision of a good standard of support for teaching activities. Some universities are the location of major national facilities, for example, the Bodleian Library in Oxford (Oxford has a quite exceptional level of expenditure) and it would be difficult to separate the local and national expenditure. Also, Bath and Manchester have national computing facilities.

Facilities spend

> *Average expenditure per student on facilities such as sports, careers services, health and counselling, from HESA data between 2001 and 2004.*

Expenditure per full-time-equivalent student on facilities such as health services, counselling, sports, recreation and others is reasonably reported for the university as a whole. However, it mostly includes central university expenditure and probably disadvantages universities with a collegiate structure.

Good honours

> *Percentage of graduates achieving a first- or upper-second-class degree, from HESA data for 2003–04.*

Universities have made little if any attempt to measure the success of their output in terms of the success of their graduates. In turn, this precludes a ranking of universities in terms of the quality of their output. The measurement of first- and upper-second-class degrees as a percentage of the total number of graduates with classified degrees has been used as a surrogate marker of the quality of teaching output from a university. However, this is naïve.

It is important to recognize that the number of firsts and upper-seconds awarded is dependent on the academic ability and application of the student. It would be extraordinary if the results from those universities with very high entrance qualifications did not partly reflect this innate academic ability. A very strong case could be made that dedicated teaching staff at universities which take students with modest A-level grades have achieved remarkable results with students who manage to gain a first. In brief, it is not possible to distinguish reliably the success of the student from the success of the university. To achieve a meaningful comparison of the success of a *university* by its degree-class output would require either the same entry-level ability of all students (clearly not possible) or a measure of 'value added'. Therefore to use degree-class output as a surrogate marker of a university's teaching success is wholly unsafe.

Graduate prospects

Percentage of a university's UK graduates in 'graduate' employment or further study, from HESA data for 2003–04. Only occupations that normally need a degree were included.

This rating relates to the ability of a university to produce a graduate who will more readily find appropriate graduate-acceptable employment. It is calculated by the number of graduates who take up employment or further study divided by the total number of graduates with a known destination, expressed as a percentage. The results are adjusted to take account of subject mix at the university. This rating implies that universities that produce graduates who have difficulty gaining employment have set lower standards or, worse, may have Mickey Mouse degree programmes that are not truly 'higher education'.

The employability of graduates is exceedingly important, since many graduates enter higher education to enhance their career prospects. However, to use it reliably to rank the teaching capability and courses of universities would require:

- that graduates from all subject areas are equally distributed throughout the university system; and

- that employers view students from all universities in an even-handed manner.

The latter point is a broad subject that needs to be examined in more detail (see Chapter 11). With regard to the former, much depends, not on the university, nor even on the student, but on the subject. It is acknowledged that the ranking values were constructed to take account of subject mix, but differences in terms of employment prospects are huge. Unsurprisingly, medical schools score maximum or near maximum points, as do schools of veterinary science, pharmacy, nursing, optometry and other healthcare subjects, while others languish at below the 50-per-cent mark.

Completion

> *Percentage of students at each university who are expected to graduate, including those who transfer to other institutions to complete courses, mainly from HESA data for 2003–04 and earlier years.*

The main reasons why students fail to complete their course, or are delayed, are either withdrawal from the course or examination failure. Other reasons include student ill-health, but also possibly a poor choice by students in selecting their course, poor student motivation and application, misleading guidance by the university, and poor counselling. Low completion rates within a particular course would suggest that the course rather than the student is at fault.

A definitive guide to the best universities in Britain?

In July 2003 the *Daily Telegraph* compiled what it described as 'the definitive guide to the best universities in Britain', bringing together in a single table the university rankings published by the *Daily Telegraph*, the *Financial Times*, the *Guardian*, the *Sunday Times* and *The Times*. While this was not a definitive answer, it certainly highlighted the fact that the various newspapers had clear differences in what they believed to be important in designing their tables. Criteria ranged in number from 6 to 17, with weightings varying from table to table. The *Daily Telegraph* focused only on teaching quality; some papers included research ratings, others did not.

One interesting inclusion in this 'league of leagues' was that, for the first time, it included the ranking of an opinion survey from more than 200 employers, including banks, management consultants and manufacturers, who regularly recruit graduates. Since employers are on the receiving end of what universities produce – the fully fledged graduate – their opinion of how well or otherwise universities do their job is of great interest, not least to the student and employee-to-be (see Chapter 11).

As with all such statistical data, the information provides a snap shot in time and problems in the past may have been transitory, and are now corrected or may be persisting. However, it becomes clear that the interpretation of university league tables requires considerable care. Students need to read beyond the averages and the rankings drawn from a multiplicity of criteria. They need to seek out evidence of the quality of the teaching and learning environment for a particular course and university best suited to their individual requirements. Such evidence was initially obtained from the impartial external audit undertaken by the Teaching Quality Agency; the TQA has subsequently been phased out (see Chapters 5 and 6). *The Times* Good University Guide was surely correct in saying that the acceptance by the Government of the universities' case for scrapping the onerous assessment system would deprive candidates of valuable information and leave a hole in the rankings. Professor Derek Bok, formerly president of Harvard University, has emphasised that 'no reliable method yet exists that allows students to determine where they will learn the most... Indeed, students often flock to courses with superficial appeal or to institutions with established reputations even though the education they receive is only mediocre.'[8]

Rigging the market

Difficulties in the interpretation of rankings reflect a global problem. For example, in America the USNews.com (www.usnews.com/usnews/edu) published on 20 August 2004 the ranking criteria and weightings of 'America's Best Colleges 2005'. Some criteria are analogous to those used in ranking higher-education institutions in the UK: SAT or ACT scores on entry, student–faculty ratios, retention rates and expenditure per student. But additional criteria include the number of alumni donating money, the average faculty pay, and peer assessment. These are alien to the UK rankings. But the American experience, with intense competition between colleges and universities, reveals the temptation that exists for even some of the most selective colleges and universities to manipulate or cheat with the rankings.

For example, Professor David Kirp highlighted one manoeuvre which he described as 'rigging the market': 'Since the "rate of giving" (donations) by alumni is factored into the U.S.News & World Report rankings, some universities, Cornell among them, simply eliminate from their data base graduates who are not likely to donate by reclassifying them as deceased.'[9]

Schools have also been known to fudge the numbers in reporting their students' SAT scores. In 1995 the *Wall Street Journal* compared the SAT scores that universities reported to bond agencies with those they provided to U.S. News. About 20 per cent of the time there were notable discrepancies, with the U.S.News figures almost always higher.[10]

Steve Stecklow relates that 'Edward Hershey, the former director of communications at Colby College, recalled how administrators there "huddled at a meeting that could only be described as a strategy session on how to cheat on the system". When the school "mistakenly" reported 80 per cent, rather than 60 per cent of Colby's freshmen were in the top 10 per cent of their high school class... Colby jumped to 15th place from 20th place in the [U.S.News] rankings. "The downside was that we spent the year figuring out how to play with some other numbers to preserve our competitive advantage."'[11]

The National Student Survey

In 2005 there appeared a form of ranking of an entirely new sort, one based on what final-year students thought about the course they had followed at any university in England, Wales and Northern Ireland. This first National Student Survey (NSS) brought together, institution by institution and course by course, the responses of 170,000 students (60 per cent of those eligible) to 22 statements, including: 'Staff have made the subject interesting'; 'Feedback on my work has been prompt'; 'I have received sufficient advice and support with my studies'; 'The course is well organised and is running smoothly'. Overall satisfaction was also assessed.

The importance of the survey was immediately obvious: it identified the institutions and courses that final-year students thought were best and worst with respect to teaching and learning. And surely they should know. In turn it offered prospective students far more information and, more importantly, more relevant information about each university's performance than they had ever had before. Hannah Essex, vice-president of education for the National Union of Students, which supports what has become an annual survey said: 'The National Student Survey gives final-year students a unique opportunity to inform future students about the quality of their student experience.'[12] Bill Rammell, the higher education minister at the time, claimed: 'This is about empowering students. Over time, the [National Student Survey] website will identify those institutions and courses that are not coming up to scratch and force them to change or close. Students will want to know that the investment they are making represents the best value for their money. This knowledge will put them in a strong position to bring about further improvements in courses and institutions.'[13]

The survey was also welcomed by Sir Martin Harris, director of the Office for Fair Access: 'It will help prospective students to make better informed choices about what and where to study.' Sir Howard Newby, chief executive of the Higher Education Funding Council for England, which ran the survey with the National Union of Students, commented: 'When you look into the data, you will find a lot of surprises. Less fashionable institutions come out of this extremely well.'[14]

The usual university league table rankings were indeed turned on their head. On a scale of 1 to 5, the highest-rated university for overall satisfaction was the Open University, scoring 4.5, followed by Birkbeck (which caters exclusively for part-time mature students), Leicester and Loughborough, all with scores of 4.3. The 'prestige' research universities appeared towards the middle of the pile when ranked in terms of student satisfaction.

Welcoming the OU's results across all subjects, Brenda Gourley, its vice-chancellor, could afford to be modest, saying: 'Our students are often making quite a sacrifice by taking on a degree while working. For this reason, they tell us if they are dissatisfied with anything and we act on it.' Carolyn Price, head of the OU's department of philosophy, said: 'We have been careful about responding to students' needs.'

An OU student, Tim Brokker, provides an unusual commendation of the strengths of the OU. In an article entitled 'I could be online with my class while in my bunker', by Jessica Shepherd, the former Royal Navy helicopter technician recounts how he was stationed on HMS Invincible off the coast of Iraq for the first year of his undergraduate degree with the Open University, but had 'every bit the student experience' because of the ease with which he could contact tutors and fellow students. Mr Brokker, who graduated with a 2:1 in June 2005, is quoted as saying: 'I am not surprised at how well the Open University has done in this survey. I haven't a bad word to say about it. The tutors tried to make it as easy as possible for me to study in the middle of a war zone. The student support is excellent. The technology used by the university makes a big difference. I could be online with my class while in my bunker and could e-mail essays to my tutors in the middle of the night.' Mr Brokker went on to Exeter University to train to be a secondary school history teacher. 'Distance learning may not be for everybody,' he said. 'You have to be quite independent, have good time management and be a lateral thinker. I wouldn't have chosen anywhere else for my first degree.'[15]

Data from the NSS was rapidly assimilated into the *Sunday Times* University League Table, along with the newspaper's own survey of head teachers' opinions.[16] The inclusion of the heads' assessments is interesting. After all, the advice given to students in secondary schools by the heads and their teachers may powerfully influence student choice of course and university. The *Sunday Times* sought the views of more than a 1,000 head teachers at Britain's leading state and independent schools; just under 250 responded.[17] The heads were asked to identify the highest quality undergraduate provision across 30 subject areas, but they were asked to cite only universities and subjects that they felt comfortable with *from their direct experience*. The inevitable patchiness of this assessment is a fatal flaw, but the mismatches in perception were sometimes dramatic (see Tables 4.2 and 4.3).

A comparison of the perceptions of 250 head teachers of the 'highest quality undergraduate teaching' and that of 170,000 undergraduate students in the National Student Survey 2005

Table 4.2 Top and bottom 5 universities according to NSS 2005

	University	NSS data (scale range 3.5–5.0)*	Head teachers' score (scale range 0–50)
1	Open University	4.16	–
2	St Mary's University College	4.04	1
3	Loughborough	4.03	13
4	Leicester	4.00	7
5	East Anglia	3.95	10
89	Greenwich	3.62	1
90	Middlesex	3.56	1
91	Brunel	3.55	9
92	University of the Arts, London	3.53	18
93	London Metropolitan	3.5	–

Where no figure is given in the head teachers' assessment, this indicates a nil response.
* Mean of the NSS 'teaching' and 'assessment and feedback' scores, calculated by the *Times Higher Education Supplement* 25 September 2005.
Source: National Student Survey 2005 and *Sunday Times*

Table 4.3 Top 10 universities according to head teachers

	University	Head teachers' score	NSS teaching/ assessment and feedback scores (mean)
1	Cambridge	46	–*
2	Oxford	41	–*

Table **4.3** Continued

	University	Head teachers' score	NSS teaching/ assessment and feedback scores (mean)
3	Imperial College London	35	3.72
4	Bristol	31	3.82
5	Bath	29	3.76
6	LSE	28	3.82
7	King's College London	25	3.85
8	Durham	24	3.90
= 8	Warwick	24	_*
10	Nottingham	23	3.79

* were not included in NSS (see text)

Source: National Student Survey 2005 and *Sunday Times*

In general, the universities rated most highly by the head teachers appeared in the middle of the NSS ranking: only Durham, Exeter and Loughborough appeared in the top 20 in both. A notable observation is that seven of the London institutions occupied ten of the bottom places in the student rankings. In particular, the University of the Arts London, successful in the survey of head teachers' opinion (ranking 16th position), returned one of the lowest scores in the students' ranking.

Thus, prospective students have an interesting dilemma. Do they believe the assessment of 250 head teachers or the collective views of 170,000 final-year undergraduate students who were actually on the receiving end of the university undergraduate education? David Eastwood, vice-chancellor of the University of East Anglia, whose university also did well in the first survey, said that few universities will be able to rest on their laurels, and he predicted considerable variation in the results each year. 'Even a few different answers next year could change the score for a university considerably,' he said. 'The survey's underlying message is that overall students are pretty satisfied. But universities across the country will be looking at the results and seeking to improve them by next year.'[18] However, the results for 2006 and 2007 were similar to 2005. The *Times Higher Education Supplement* scores indicate that the University of Buckingham (private) entered the survey in 2006 and (with an exceptional staff–student ratio) ranked first. The Open University came second. The University of Oxford entered the survey in 2007 coming second, with the Open University coming third. The students in all three years remained unsatisfied with their feedback.[19]

For prospective students, their parents and teachers, as well as academic staff and admissions officers, the NSS, now in its third year, provides an important source of information in the choice of university and course.

Chapter 5

The Research Effect

The Research Effect

TEACHING AND RESEARCH have come to be seen as the core dual functions of a university, but it has not always been so. In the nineteenth century Cardinal Newman asserted that the university was 'a place of teaching universal knowledge... with the diffusion and extension of knowledge rather than its advancement. If its object were scientific and philosophical discovery, I do not see why a University should have students'.[1] In brief, universities were about teaching, not research. It is only in the last hundred years that research became a function of universities and, finally, the major driving force, at least in older or 'prestige' universities.

Research is of obvious relevance to certain stakeholders in higher education: the Government, the tax-payers, the academic institutions and their staff. Original discoveries in the sciences may lead to patents, commercialisation and, finally, financial benefits to the nation. This may be more difficult to achieve within the humanities, but their vital role as social entrepreneurs can benefit society in profound ways. For many, the inescapable daily exposure to the ills of a fractured society is revealing that social rather than economic concerns are the greater priority. Most academics do not do research primarily to make money. Far more rewarding for most academics is the joy of discovery and the respect of one's peer group. To make a fortunate discovery that may benefit or make a difference to society is, as I know from experience, the most rewarding of all.

But this is not necessarily the view of some academic institutions and their bureaucratic leadership, for whom Research is the new academic god. Many universities are focused on the next Research Assessment Exercise with a fear and compulsion that verge on the pathological; and the five billion pounds of tax-payers' money that will be distributed on the back of the exercise commands a myopic focus for many universities. Their behaviour has been changed and is now controlled by the exercise.

Does this have any real relevance for students themselves, either in their choice of university or the quality of education they receive? Most certainly, not least because balancing the importance between teaching and research is one of the most sensitive issues in higher education today: and the issue is whether or not the focus on research may distract universities and their staff from their teaching responsibilities. For someone primarily concerned with the quality of undergraduate teaching – the student – there is a disturbing pattern of evidence. This pattern has been evident to the academic community world-wide for decades[2] but whilst the problems are international, they have been exacerbated in this country by the introduction of the Research Assessment Exercise.

The Research Assessment Exercise

A Research Selectivity Exercise was introduced by the University Grants Committee (UGC) in 1981 in response to demands by government for a greater accountability for UGC grants given for academic research. The exercise was redesignated in 1986 as the Research Assessment Exercise (RAE) because its original title was thought to misrepresent its true intent. The exercise was designed to support and improve the quality of research in the universities in a selective manner. Academics and universities were to be ranked in terms of 'research excellence', with ratings familiar to all staff. As a result the RAE gradings and ranking have become the single most important factor in institutional prestige, a vital source of income and a magnet for additional research funding from the research councils, charities, industry and elsewhere. There have been determined attempts to enhance university research, with departments and universities orchestrating their submissions with exquisite care to gain maximum benefit from the ranking exercise. But there is a dark and humourless side to the RAE which is recognised far beyond the walls of academe.

The next RAE is due in 2008. At the time of the last one, in 2001, an editorial in *The Times* began:

> Albert Camus described an intellectual as 'someone whose mind watches itself'. In the contemporary British university, alas, the minds of most academics are occupied by considerations of funds and bureaucracy. The deadline for submission under the RAE ended yesterday – an endeavour which has cost £40 million and which will determine the fate of about £5 billion in public money. Entire departments may expand, decline or even disappear depending on the

decisions which will be announced this December. It has long been clear that the RAE involves an almost crushing burden of paperwork. This could be justified if it led to a rational distribution of resources. The RAE seems instead to be a hugely distorting enterprise... The underlying problem is that in many disciplines it is extremely difficult, if not completely impossible to create objective standards for comparing scholarship. The quest for common procedure has meant that an admittedly imperfect system of peer group review through research councils has been devoured by the monster that is the RAE.

The editorial concluded:

The breathing space before the next RAE should prompt the Department for Education to conduct a fundamental review of the entire procedure. Although most complaints have been directed, understandably, against the paperwork linked with the RAE, this is not the critical question. A less bureaucratic structure which still distorted academic research would not represent a meaningful improvement... It is time for the exercise itself to be the subject of searching assessment.[3]

If researchers are no longer regarded as valued colleagues but as a purchasable commodity for their money and ranking, 'buying' them with promises of reduced teaching loads and more money perfectly describes the new moral low ground to be found in the prestigious swamps of higher education. Even Nobel Prize winners can be reduced to a commodity: one university has purchased one and requires another four. Any offers? Does this behaviour enhance or degrade an institution?

The serious nature of the problem and how research 'success' can adversely affect undergraduate teaching is evident in the views expressed by influential establishment bodies or individuals. In his Royal Society anniversary address in December 2003, the president of the Society, Lord Robert May, questioned universities' insistence that research was a prerequisite for good teaching. Lord May said the argument that research and teaching must be kept together was 'supported by repeated assertion and little else'. He accused universities of a 'widely held piety' that a faculty must be research-active to provide good teaching, although he added the claim that good researchers made the best teachers, an assertion that is in fact intensely controversial and may also be 'supported by repeated assertion and little else'. He suggested that the four-year teaching-only colleges in the USA provided a sound model for the UK: 'The graduates of the best of these are not handicapped.' Lord May called for the RAE to be scrapped, and warned that teaching was being overshadowed by research: 'It is arguably becoming almost a mark of status to have minimum contact with undergraduates. This is clearly bad for a university.'[4]

Sir Howard Newby, chief executive of the Higher Education Funding Council for England until January 2006, also expressed serious concern at the status of teaching:

> I do hope there will be institutions that focus on teaching excellence as there are in the US. We have to reinvent teaching as being a very honourable vocation that needs to be rewarded. Parents and students paying higher fees are not going to be content if all that money is going into strengthening the research element of universities.[5]

Meanwhile, Sir Harry Kroto, professor of chemistry at Sussex University, and Nobel prizewinner for chemistry in 1996, was worried about the RAE effect as he championed chemistry as a field where individuals and small groups could still make a massive impact:

> We should use the RAE as an incentive and find imaginative ways to strengthen the research and teaching capabilities of our universities. But I fear that many vice-chancellors are all too ready to use it to justify a slash and burn policy in the UK's traditional heartland. If research disappears from our smaller universities, and is concentrated in half a dozen or so ponderous battleships, it will be goodbye to the sort of laboratories where some of the UK's finest chemistry has been done; where the molecules that made liquid crystal displays possible were designed, where genetic fingerprinting was invented, where the measurements that revealed the structure of DNA were made.[6]

University research, the undergraduate and the halo effect

Few in academia would disagree that the undergraduate students should have a greater exposure to, and involvement in, an understanding of research. In the words of the Higher Education Council of Australia: 'Perhaps the most important "generic" skill that a graduate can possess is the ability to recognise that knowledge is provisional, and that no answer is final, and that there is always potential for a better way of doing things.[7]

In view of the emphasis placed on research by government and tax-payers, the academic institutions and their staff, should the research standing of a university be relevant to an undergraduate student's education and influence their initial choice of institution? The answer is yes, but a guarded yes. There are both direct and indirect ways in which research can positively influence, or at least be of potential value to, the undergraduate:

- *direct*: where research staff or facilities contribute to undergraduate teaching and learning activities. To be of distinctive value, the contribution of research or research-and-teaching staff would be required to be at a level, experience or presentation not attainable by the 'teaching-only' staff;

- *indirect*: where the reputation as a 'research university' has the effect of attracting high-quality students (or at least those with high A level grades) and conferring, via a halo effect, a badge of excellence on the emerging graduate.[8]

The indirect influence is of considerable importance to a student. The external (and frequently internal) perception of the reputation of older universities is largely related to their research strengths. Employers may preferentially seek out research universities to locate future employees, not because of the research but because these universities attract students with good A-level grades (and therefore potentially good minds). For the student, enhancing the opportunity of future employment is a vital issue, so it would seem to make sense to aim for universities where employers are likely to look first. A self-feeding circle is created but, as we shall see, not necessarily a virtuous circle.

The 'excellent at research' label includes a multitude of misperceptions that universities, students and society appear only too willing to perpetuate. In their marketing, universities perceived or rated the 'top', 'best', 'highly rated' or 'prestige' for research are careful to allow students and parents to subconsciously coalesce the attribution of excellence to both the research and teaching activities, which may or may not be true. Marketing, as academics are fully aware, is about persuasion, and the warning must be 'Let the buyer beware.' This becomes particularly important when there is clear evidence that a university's research activities may indeed have relevance to the actual teaching of undergraduate students, but in unexpected and sometimes disturbing and destructive ways.

Questioning standards

The real question therefore is: how do the research activities of a university actually affect the undergraduate teaching and learning experience? Is it, in particular, improved by the presence and involvement of research staff, and is it affected by the institution's research ranking?

Are the standards of teaching enhanced by research staff in high-ranking research universities?

First, we must acknowledge that there are clear differences in opinion with respect to the relevance of research to teaching. The Government is clearly of the view that there is no necessary link between the amount of research taking place at an institution and the quality of teaching. Ministers are actually encouraging some universities to focus or specialise in teaching.

> We believe that the time has come to look carefully at the relationship between research and teaching. In reality, the connection between an institution's research activities and its teaching is indirect, and there is ample evidence of the highest quality teaching being achieved in circumstances which are not research-intensive. The scale and location of research activity has to be justified and decided on its own merits.[9]

But the rector of Imperial College, Sir Richard Sykes, a key supporter and major beneficiary of government moves to concentrate research funding on an elite minority of universities and to push some institutions into teaching-only roles, said that he did not believe that:

the highest quality of teaching can be delivered by those divorced from active engagement in research... I am sure that moves to create teaching-only institutions will result in a clearer stratification of higher education than we currently admit to.[10]

So, who is correct, Sir Richard or the ministers? The stakes are high.

If the standards of teaching are enhanced by research staff, then high-ranking research universities should show evidence of better teaching. This is not easy to ascertain, but one indicator might be the teaching standards attained by the Russell Group of 20 universities (see Appendix 2), which attracts about 60 per cent of research council funding. However, in the National Student Surveys, universities in the Russell Group generally appeared towards the middle of the rankings in student satisfaction in both 2005 and 2006 (Chapter 4). It would seem that the ministers rather than Sir Richard appear to be correct.

Is the quality of learning at universities enhanced by a high ranking in research?

At the time of the debate over the introduction of tuition fees, the Russell Group campaigned for higher student fees to reflect the quality of learning at member institutions. It also considered a preferential pay structure to attract 'top academics'. These are distinct but related issues and of vital importance to undergraduate students when they are being requested to foot the bill! For students may find themselves being in the future requested to pay extra fees to a Russell Group university for the privilege of paying 'top academics' greater salaries, and to reflect the 'quality of learning' at these institutions. But they will then be entitled to ask what is the definition of a 'top academic' and what is the quality of learning? These are questions that lie at the heart of the tensions between teaching and research.

'Top academics' could be teachers or researchers or both. A 'top researcher' could be identified on the basis of success in research grants, publications and other ratings. How is a student to assess whether such success has enhanced their own quality of learning? It would be fascinating to see objective evidence to support the hypothesis that the quality of learning is greater in research universities than in other institutions, but, as we have seen above, at present it does not appear to exist. And how exactly do you identify the best teachers? In 2005 the Government established a funding initiative involving £315 million to support 70 centres for excellence in teaching and learning (CETLs), but this has stalled or 'largely failed to develop new ways to reward and recognise good teaching'.[11]

In the USA and Australia, where they have a longer experience of paying for university education, measurements of student ratings of undergraduate teaching and research productivity show that, at best, the link between teaching and research is tenuous, if not a myth.[12] Indeed, in a study of 200 US four-year undergraduate colleges measuring student development[13] it was concluded that 'a college whose faculty is research-orientated increases student dissatisfaction and impacts negatively on most measures of cognitive and affective development'. In a subsequent study the few institutions that did score highly on both 'teaching' and 'research' were rich, private colleges.[14] Professor Gibbs, in reviewing the evidence, commented that 'despite 30 years of research there is no support for the view or belief that quality in research is necessary or even supportive of teaching'.[15] And Ruth Neumann, interviewing a range of undergraduate and postgraduate students in a large Australian research university, found that 'up-to-date knowledge and interest in the subject were not seen as substitutes for good teaching practice'.[16]

There is also evidence from the USA that fewer faculties of 'research universities' believe that their institutions are excellent in preparing undergraduates for a vocation or career, in serving non-traditional-age students effectively, in providing undergraduates with a general education, or in monitoring the academic progress of their undergraduate students. Also, fewer faculties from research universities believe strongly in the personal importance of teaching to undergraduate students. But more research faculties agree strongly that to be a good teacher one must be engaged in research and that in research universities the pressure to publish reduces the quality of teaching![17] It would be of interest to conduct a similar survey in the UK.

In their book *Reshaping teaching in higher education: linking teaching with research* (2003), Professor Alan Jenkins and colleagues emphasise the longstanding and controversial nature of this issue.[18] Whilst numerous institutional mission statements see good teaching as closely related to quality research, this is brought into doubt by the evidence and increasingly questioned by the student body. Indeed, staff commitment to research may be seen as an irrelevance or even an obstacle to improving teaching quality. The Cooperative Institutional Research Program (CIRP) initiated at the American Council on Education (ACE) in 1966, with longitudinal data covering a remarkable 11 million students and a national sample of more than 1,800 institutions of all types, has consistently shown the disadvantageous effects of a faculty with a research orientation.[19] Students' positive expression is for a faculty with a teaching orientation.

The fifth report of the House of Commons Education and Skills Committee on the future of higher education (2002–03) concluded that:

> We believe it is important for the quality of students' educational experience that research should continue to be undertaken in higher education institutions. This does not mean that all institutions should seek to emulate the research intensive universities, or that all teachers need to be engaged in cutting edge research, but that teaching should take place in a research active environment.[20]

They reminded the Government that:

> UK universities are attractive because of their reputation for quality and excellence, much of which is rooted in their unique blend of teaching and research. We warn the government not understanding the distinctive nature of our university system or failing to maintain its quality would be a fundamental mistake.[21]

In summary, the answer to our question is: the research activities of a university play a pivotal role in establishing institutional prestige and may contribute to a positive educational ambience for undergraduate students, but no evidence could be found to show that high-profile research universities provide better teaching or learning for undergraduate students.

The destructive effects of the RAE on teaching and research

There is, however, a more troubling question: can research activity actually damage the teaching experience?

The first study to look at the impact of research on teaching in the UK was undertaken in the mid-1990s by Professor Alan Jenkins from Oxford Brookes University, an internationally known expert on the relationship between teaching and research. In looking at a single discipline, geography, at 14 universities, both old and new, he concluded:

Funding and quality procedures have caused individuals (i.e. academic staff), departments and institutions to prioritise research, and given that staff time and resources are limited, to neglect teaching. There are significant financial rewards too for developing quality research. By contrast, doing well in the teaching quality exercise produces at best symbolic rewards... The study demonstrates that the RAE has had significant and largely negative impacts on the organisation of teaching and perhaps on aspects of teaching quality in these 14 geography departments. By comparison, the teaching quality assessment has made little or no impact... Everything tells you (i.e. the academic staff) to concentrate all your energies into research... Teaching needs to be seen to be judged worthwhile by universities. Appointing and promoting academics as a reward for excellence in teaching is the only way.[22]

There is little reason to doubt that the findings in geography reflected a similar picture in other subjects.

More recently, Professor Graham Gibbs, director of higher education practice based at the Open University, claimed that the RAE had contorted departmental life in institutions. He noted that departments that are research-led often let lecturers off teaching duties because of time pressures and relied on inexperienced postgraduates to take classes. He said that they also adopt policies that limit students' experiences of learning, such as dropping coursework in favour of a single exam, restricting student access to their project and dissertation supervisors, halving the number of seminars while doubling their size, or not marking lab reports. Professor Gibbs uses his two daughters' undergraduate experiences as examples of the quality of teaching students receive:

Both have experienced late feedback on assignments, very little feedback when it does arrive and, sometimes no feedback at all... The fact that my daughters' lecturers are at the cutting edge of their subject when undertaking their research does not help my daughters that much in relation to the feedback they do not receive. [23]

But it would be wrong to place the blame for the distortion in the balance of teaching and research entirely at the door of the RAE. Academics have traditionally entered a university career as an almost unique opportunity for researching and teaching, and usually in that order. That many university academics prefer research to teaching is an accepted fact, and the RAE has probably only exposed the inherent culture to prioritise research rather than teaching.

The damage to teaching

In the wake of the results of the RAE 2001, and the way funding followed research rankings, came a devastating erosion of departmental and institutional respect for non-research activities, including teachers and teaching. A craven obedience to the research rankings directly influenced the teaching role and therefore the academic staff and undergraduate students.

First, and perhaps the worst excess of the RAE, was the attempted separation of academic staff into research 'active' and 'non-active' divisions. In what is perhaps higher education's darkest hour, 'academic cleansing' then followed. The reputation of universities as institutions of tolerance, generosity and understanding disintegrated. Those academic disciplines and their staff that did not meet arbitrary research criteria designated as worthy of support were culled, irrespective of the teaching expertise. The ensuing outcry hit the headlines time and again (see box).

Respect for the teaching function and teachers was reduced to an all-time low. Some dedicated and most distinguished teachers with decades of experience simply left in disgust. The views in a letter to the editor of *The Times* in June 2003 were shared by many academic staff:

> You report that the system of ranking and funding university department research is to be reformed. It is a pity that the whole system is not going to be scrapped. The pressure on academics to conduct research has become so intense due to the prestige, rankings and funding which research attracts, that university teaching has become devalued and disregarded. Many, if not most, university academics now try to do as little teaching as possible, or even attempt to avoid teaching entirely, so that they can maximise time for research. University lecturers who do still take teaching seriously are sneered at by their colleagues, or are liable to be told that they are not 'not a serious academic' (as

I was last year, by a professorial colleague). Research is now an obsession in universities and the only real criterion of appointment or promotion. It does not matter how badly you teach, or whether you do any teaching at all, as long as you keep churning out ever more books, articles and conference papers. Students and parents would be disgusted if they realised the contempt with which many, if not most, academics now view teaching. If I had known just how much teaching would become devalued in Britain's universities I would not have entered academia 15 years ago. Now I am just looking forward to early retirement.

Peter Dorey
Senior Lecturer in Politics
Cardiff University[24]

This culling process, however, has also on occasion rebounded on the university. In February 2005 the Medical Research Council announced that the prestigious National Institute for Medical Research – which has produced five Nobel prizewinners – would move to University College London. For months, King's College London had been pitched against UCL to secure this ground-breaking merger. Council members told the *Times Higher Education Supplement* that the closure of King's chemistry department had been the deal breaker for King's. Michael Wakelam, professor of molecular pharmacology at Birmingham University and a member of the MRC said: 'There is a clear lesson for universities here. If you look at the most successful science based universities in this country, they have a wide breadth of science.' He confirmed that while King's was very impressive, its decision to close its chemistry department had been a key reason for declining its bid.[25]

The damage to research

Research excellence as recognised by the RAE (which defines it in terms of national or international importance) has become an ever-refining focus on narrower and narrower research themes. In turn research themes and research groups have been imaginatively created or contrived by universities in a way that leads to success in the RAE.

Moves to move up the RAE rankings

Newspaper reports from just a few months of 2003 and 2004 give an indication of the effects of the intense focus on the RAE.

June 2003 Oxford University history department has recently been downgraded from 5* to 5. The chairman of the faculty board says that diverting staff from teaching into research is the only way to regain the department's star rating.[26]

July 2003 Cambridge is reported to be axing its Part II diploma in architecture. The first sign that something was wrong came with the results of the 2001 RAE which saw the school fall from a 5-star to 4 rating, depriving it of more than £200,000 of research funding... On 29 November a 1,000 strong demonstration by Cambridge students and supporters protested against the closure of the architecture department.[27]

June 2004 Following a review of the sustainability of creative arts at Lancaster University, the university plans to axe its art department and focus on music and theatre studies. The art department scored a 3a in the 2001 RAE whereas the music and theatre studies research was awarded a 4 ranking. It was hoped that investing cash in the 4-ranking department would help them secure a 5 or 5*-rating in the next RAE in 2008.[28]

June 2004 Aberdeen University is to shed about 80 posts as part of a long-term strategy of the university to focus more resources on courses and subjects where recruitment is healthy and which score well in the RAE.[29]

The same editorial in The Times that was so highly critical of the RAE 2001 (see above) also reported on two phenomena observed as a result of the demands of the exercise: the rise of a 'transfer market' among academics, and an avalanche of hurried publications. If a high-starred research academic can be lured away from one university to another, then an enhanced salary or promise of fewer lectures is a small price to pay for the potentially massive return in extra funding that an improved research rating will attract. Equally, publication is an easily demonstrable form of research activity, and academics (and academic publishers) have witnessed a huge increase in publications, some extremely obscure, in a bid to score RAE points. As a counter to this, *The Times* reported, there has been a considerable reduction in books written by academics for the student market: 'If even a small number of Dons have been discouraged from writing books for an audience wider than a select band of fellow specialists then this is an unacceptable price to pay for bureaucratic neatness.'

Norman Stone, professor of modern history at Oxford 1984–97, was less kind:

> The whole research assessment exercise is a farce… We are already swimming in unreadable articles. The journals are read by the author, his mother and a bureaucrat, and that's it. The university should throw the whole exercise in the bin and become independent. It's ridiculous to cut back on the thing they do best: teaching.[30]

Janet Lewis, former research director of the Joseph Rowntree Foundation and member of the social policy and social work panel for the 2001 RAE, expressed similar views and concluded that in its present form the RAE had outlived its usefulness:

> Benefits of the exercise were identified as raising the profile of research in some universities… But a whole range of dysfunctional aspects were also identified. It operated a 'one size-fits-all' model, despite considerable differences between disciplines and the huge diversity between institutions and in the types of research being carried out. But at least as important is the range of unintended consequences; the gamesmanship around identifying who is 'research active', people seeking funds who have little talent for research, the proliferation of small-circulation journals on esoteric subjects.[31]

This 'one size fits all' approach of which Janet Lewis complained, with the RAE structured overwhelmingly on research within highly focused disciplines, inevitably perpetuated departmental and institutional isolation and focused on 'academic' research, with a relatively poor recognition of the value of an individual's research. After Herculean efforts, many academics, having attained coveted RAE grades, found there was no financial support for their endeavours.[32]

Perhaps the real tragedy of the RAE is the latest attempts of universities to restrict funding even further to just a few groups of researchers, which may actually reduce rather than enhance research as a whole. Damning comments from no less than 30 chairs of the RAE panels (accounting for about half of all chairs) have been reported [33] and the House of Commons Education and Skills Select Committee also recorded deep concern that 'the scientists are frightened to stand up and be critical'.[34] The scientists, however, may have decided that enough is enough, as the boxed text indicates.

David Campbell, professor of geography at Durham University, sums up the need for a new attitude to research:

> The whole point of working in a university is being able to explore your own intellectual agenda. Our vice-chancellor has said he wants our university to become the Princeton of Europe. If you look at what they measure at Princeton in terms of the performance of academics, you will find the answer is nothing. They just recruit good people and let them get on with it.[35]

The RAE: a fatally flawed exercise?

The next review, RAE 2008, is underway. Have lessons been learnt, or are the same damaging mistakes being perpetuated?

The revamped RAE starting in 2007 has already made a mockery of the independence of the Higher Education Funding Council for England and bestows riches partly on the basis of work submitted almost a decade ago.[36] With 5* or 6* ratings, stars appear to emanate from every orifice. The Royal Society has made its views plain: it is calling for the Government to scrap the RAE in favour of a 'profile-based system'. It wants the Government to recognise that it is individuals and not departments who undertake research, and that excellent researchers should be supported regardless of location.[37]

Counting research achievements like beans

Scientists acknowledge they are accountable in post. But they have also begun to acknowledge their professional obligation to the tax-payer, their science and society. The initial focus of their attack has been on the disastrous attempts at measuring the quality of their research.

Teaching and administrative duties can readily be assessed through the nature of the duties and number of contact hours. But research is a different animal. This can only be realistically assessed by other researchers who have an expert knowledge of the field. At Imperial College London, internationally respected for the quality of its research, staff have been provided with a 'productivity' target for publications: three papers a year. A 'publication score' is then calculated, taking into account the prestige of the journal in which they have published, how many co-authors were involved, and how far up (or down) their name appears in the credits for a multi-authored work. A circulated annual spreadsheet announces each researcher's publication score, along with financial viability. On his website www.goodscience.org.uk David Colquhoun, professor of pharmacology at UCL, scorns the validity of the scoring system from his personal experience and that of his colleagues, and discovers that Nobel prize-winners may fail the 'quality control' test – which says it all.[38]

One could seriously question the value of the RAE or any other such contrivance as the most effective mechanism for the development of 'creative and novel' research. Universities UK has reviewed the evidence for focusing research and concludes that 'the grade 4 units appear to be competitive in international terms and continue to make a substantial contribution to the UK's overall research performance'.[39] Also, it is estimated that the jobs of at least 8,000 staff in 500 grade-4 departments are under threat.[40]

The RAE has seen the creation of an ever-increasing and parochial focus by individual institutions, their vice-chancellors and senior administrative colleagues desperately attempting to improve finances within their own institutions. This has been undertaken with no interest in or understanding for the potentially disastrous effect of the sum total of these haphazard changes on different subject areas.

In this chapter we have seen how research may influence teaching and teaching staff in universities. But rather than supporting teaching, a focus on research has frequently had the perverse effect of relegating the teaching role to secondary importance in some of our most eminent universities. It is most unlikely that some of the views expressed by some of the universities in this chapter will ever be repeated. They may be perceived as dangerously revealing of true and destructive intent.

It has been suggested, and at a global level,[41] that the renewed focus on undergraduate education is probably the most pressing issue that universities must face in the next decade. The challenge is to demonstrate that the learning and research environments at the undergraduate level are not competitive but complementary. But without a strong research base, it is unlikely that the all-important teaching–research nexus will be achieved.

Chapter 6

Teaching, Learning and Earning:
Degrees of Dilemma

Teaching, Learning and Earning: Degrees of Dilemma

STUDENTS AND PARENTS may be surprised (or disbelieving) to read that few university academics possess a teaching qualification, or that UK universities have, as Professor Alan Jenkins of Oxford Brookes University put it, a 'large part-time army that now does much of the teaching'. Most academics were primarily appointed on the basis of their research potential; it was just assumed that they could, or would learn to, teach.

The absence of a teaching credential does not appear to have disadvantaged the academic staff in their interaction and involvement with undergraduate students, or the efforts of some to improve the quality of their teaching. The teaching styles of tens of thousands of teachers will inevitably reflect their knowledge and life experience. It is perhaps by their all-important daily example, their concern, their kindness, together with their all-important human failings, rather than by their instruction, that students will remember them from their university days, with pleasure and amusement.

Teachers in higher education normally try desperately hard to educate rather than simply engage in the routine of course delivery. The modular system, however, in fractionating learning, has a great deal to answer for. The immense pressures on students to 'learn to the examination' are a further hindrance. But perhaps the greatest pressure placed on teachers has been the 'academic cleansing' that has taken place because of the focus on research (see Chapter 5). The National Committee of Inquiry into Higher Education in 1997 (the Dearing Report) emphasised the importance of improvements in teaching standards. It proposed the setting up of a new professional body, the Institute for Learning and Teaching (ILT). The ILT had a troubled history and became defunct. The Higher Education Academy (HEA) took over its role to improve the student experience, to raise the status of teaching and learning and to recognise the place of teaching and learning in career development. It has been a difficult journey. The developing frameworks are still perceived to separate teaching and research, and ignore the needs of the 'large part-time army that now does much of the teaching', referred to by Professor Jenkins. According to Peter Hartley, professor of education development at Bradford University: 'The

ILT was proactive in terms of banging the drum to make teaching and learning more central to university life. The HEA hasn't done that yet.'[1]

However, in August 2007 the HEA announced a new development was to 'initiate a programme of work to develop a systematic approach to the use of teaching excellence as a criterion on a par with research excellence for promotion to the highest academic posts'. Perhaps, just perhaps, this is finally the occasion for change?[2]

Student–staff ratios

According to the latest statistics from the Higher Education Funding Council for England (HEFCE) for 2005-06, there are 162,895 full- and part-time academic staff involved in teaching or research. Of these about a quarter are described as 'teaching only' (of which most, just over 80 per cent, are part-time). Almost another quarter (23 per cent) are 'research only' (but about 80 per cent are full-time appointments). This leaves slightly over half (51 per cent), who are described as 'teaching and research', and the majority of these (82 per cent) are full-time.

A perhaps unsettling fact to emerge from these figures is the major contribution to teaching by part-time staff. In some disciplines this may relate to the use of highly experienced practitioners to build upon the academic teaching and learning. However, it may also relate to 'an army of postgraduate and postdoctoral students in old universities who shoulder much of the teaching burden'.[3] Some of the experience these postgraduates gain is obviously important in preparation for subsequent academic careers, but data from the Higher Education Policy Institute show that close to 30 per cent of seminars and tutorials in pre-1992 universities are led by non-academics. The bulk of practical

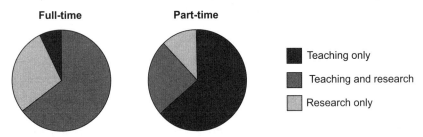

Full-time   **Part-time**

■ Teaching only

■ Teaching and research

□ Research only

Figure 6.1   Roles of academic staff 2005–06

Source: HEFCE

supervision, such as laboratory work, also falls to non-academics in both old and new universities.[4] A third alternative is that some of these part-time teachers may be academic staff on short-term contracts to minimise the financial costs of teaching. However, the Association of University Teachers and the lecturers' union, NATFHE, now merged as the Universities and Colleges Union, is committed to prevent the 'disgusting exploitation' and 'casualisation' of part-time and hourly paid lecturers.[5]

Previous data from the Higher Education Statistics Agency (HESA) for 1995–96 recorded 'teaching only' staffing as 11,734; 'teaching and research' as 70,469; 'research only' as 32,518; providing a total staffing of 114,719. Therefore the total staffing (teaching and research) within a decade has increased by 42 per cent. But the 1995–96 data did not report the part-time staffing numbers which is vital to compare the figures properly. The figures such as they are should be compared to a potted summary of a decade of achievements in higher education from 1997 to 2007: universities' total income increased from £11.517 billion to £19.503 billion; universities' funding council income increased from £4.507 billion to £7.544 billion; universities' research grants and contracts income increased from £1.733 billion to £3.121 billion; student numbers increased from 1,800,065 to 2,287,540.[6]

Increases in the number of staff teaching our students fail to compensate for the greater student numbers now taught. HESA data between 2000–01 and 2003–04, confirms that the average student–staff ratio (SSR) in higher education increased from 16:1 in 2000–01 to more than 18:1 in 2003–04. Students outnumber academics by more than 30 to 1 at some institutions. In 2005–06, SSR data from HESA indicates a UK average of 16.8:1, which includes 'atypical' staff and further education students, but excludes research-only staff.[7] Pupil–teacher ratios in state schools are currently 16:1; in independent schools they are about 7:1. In November 2006 the Quality Assurance Agency finally admitted that rising undergraduate numbers combined with staffing cuts are damaging the student experience.[8]

Teaching and accountability

For decades, and in many cases for centuries, universities have been autonomous institutions and have vigorously defended their rights. Outside an institution there was no real understanding of the internal standards of teaching, and standards would inevitably vary from institution to institution.

The introduction of the Teaching Quality Agency (TQA) and the Quality Assurance Agency (QAA) was an attempt to regularise and improve teaching standards. Any such regulatory agency would be bureaucratic and occur financial costs. But the TQA had the advantage of an independent assessment that can be related to individual departments and academic institutions. It was also a valued mechanism to ensure that a university would properly support, to the best of its finite abilities, the provision to its departments. However, it also permitted an institutional comparison and this directly challenged the authority of the institutions. For the first time universities were held publicly accountable for the quality of their teaching. The Russell Group of universities demanded the abolition of external teaching-quality assessment, in defiance of ministers and students. It was reported that the group considered that quality inspectors should rely only 'on the outputs of internal audit process'. The QAA is now responsible for the quality and standards of teaching and learning (<http://www.qaa.uk>). In response, the president of the National Union of Students (NUS) is reported as saying that:

> The NUS is appalled at the suggestions from the Russell
> Group to abolish all forms of teaching-quality assurance in
> higher education. Students who are now contributing more
> than £1.6 billion to the sector need to feel confident that
> their expectations of a course will be fully met and that there
> are effective quality assurance procedures in place.[9]

But whatever the motivation of the Russell Group in seeking to abolish an independent assessment, it created a most unfortunate impression that certain universities were arrogant to the point of indifference towards the views of their students and of the UK tax-payer, crucial stakeholders in the higher education enterprise. The response of government was pitiable.

In any event, the appearance in 2005 of the first National Student Survey (NSS) provided a first attempt to determine the standards of teaching in higher education institutions in the UK as assessed by those most directly involved – the students. The outcome for the Russell Group was disappointing (see Chapter 4). In the NSS undertaken in 2006, the private University of Buckingham took part voluntarily for the first time, and its students, with an SSR of 1:9, ranked as the most satisfied.[10] Concerns raised by academic staff that students would abuse their position in a student survey by unfair criticism of individual members of academic staff appear to have been unfounded. Irresponsible expressions of a personal view on the Internet are of transitory interest and unrelated to formal assessments.

A helping hand, or debasing the value of a degree?

Staff, however, have other, far more serious, issues and concerns about teaching, learning and the credentialing process. For there are practices in higher education that might question objectivity in the assessment of students' work. The London College of Fashion, part of the University of the Arts London, launched an investigation in 2006 after a course director encouraged a tutor to increase a student's mark, with the comment: 'She is an international student so normally we would give her an allowance for that.'[11] Is this perceived as cheating, deceit or simply policy? Were UK students advised that this was the college policy? Is this an attempt to level the playing field – or something else?

Aid with language or writing difficulties is not limited to overseas students. The School of Management at Bradford University has on its website a list of approved freelance proofreaders that any student can use to check essays and assignments. The school's effective learning officer, Colin Neville, said: 'My own view of proofreaders is that the services of these are sought mainly by international students or able home students with particular difficulties with written communication.' Clearly, this is not deceitful but is it cheating, or a rational policy? Professor Alan Smithers, of the University of Buckingham, warned: 'If someone has a degree from an English university, it is taken as evidence by employers that they are fluent in English, so using proofreaders gives a misleading impression and devalues the degree.'[12]

As an MSc and PhD supervisor of both overseas and home students, and also as an external examiner in a number of universities, I know from personal experience that it is usually the case, and is expected by supervisors, that in the writing of a thesis by an overseas student one is resigned to correcting the second or even a third draft of a thesis. It has nothing to do with academic ability or application, simply the expected difficulty of a person attempting to use a sophisticated written expression in a second language. So, have my fellow supervisors and I been cheating for years? Or have we, perhaps unthinkingly, behaved in a professional manner, being pleased to honour the predicted commitment to our students.

How far can this 'helping hand' extend? Until fairly recently, copying from books and published articles was a slow business. Now, Internet access to resources such as Google and Wikipedia ensure answers to questions are just a click away. Access to model answers to exam questions and essay titles may take just a few moments longer. For the more difficult assignment, there are websites which will prepare essays for a relatively modest financial return.[13]

Presenting someone else's ideas or facts as if they are your own is a major global problem, in education as in the wider world. Under a Freedom of Information request, almost half of Britain's universities revealed a total of 6,672 incidents of plagiarism and collusion in the academic year 2003–04. The figures were released after universities themselves expressed concern about the incidence of plagiarism, as students turned to the Internet to buy essays and dissertations. At Westminster University, 707 students were found to have copied work without declaring it, the highest incidence in the survey.[14]

Revelations such as these reduce confidence in an individual student's knowledge, and question the foundations of the credentialing for all students. In short, the value of a degree is diminished. However, to focus on the student as the sole harbinger of cheating is totally misleading. Parents, teachers, academic staff, schools and universities all contribute to the problem. The problem for universities begins in secondary education.

A question of attribution

Some 20 years ago, secondary education modified the examining of pupils to include coursework and projects. At any level of education these are generally encouraged to enhance 'student self-learning': an admirable goal. However, the problem with work undertaken outside the classroom is that its authorship is unknown. When in 2005–06 the Qualifications and Curriculum Authority (QCA) surveyed more than 1,700 teachers and conducted interviews with over 400 students and 400 parents, more than 60 per cent of parents said they helped their children with GCSE coursework; 5 per cent admitted that they actually drafted it. It would be unrealistic to suppose that at least a proportion of the remaining 40 per cent of parents did not also help their children. Did the parents regard themselves as cheating or deceiving – or simply helping their child with homework, as parents have done for generations? If all parents could offer the same level of help to their children, then surely the domestic academic support would reinforce the school experience to the greater good – as the government has long requested! The obvious problem is that children receive very different levels of help, until it is not possible to distinguish the achievement of the pupil from that of family or friends.

The QCA accepts that coursework in most subjects cannot easily exist in a system which holds teachers accountable for their results by performance management and league tables. Many teachers have suggested that the pressure to improve results, which leads them to allow multiple redrafts of pupils' work, makes course assessment a farce. One said: 'I'm busy marking GCSE coursework at the moment. I know full well that vast amounts of it is cut-and-paste but I'm going to pretend I haven't noticed.' Another commented: 'The cheating is absurd. We largely write and grade our own work.'[15]

This provides the cultural background for students who are being prepared for university. So, what is the attitude of students to 'questionable behaviour' when they are at university? A study undertaken in a questionnaire assessment in two schools of pharmacy probably typifies student thinking.[16]

The full enquiry covered 12 questions, but in the following abstract just three are given as an indication of student responses.

Table 6.1 Attitudes to academic dishonesty

Do you believe the following to be wrong:		School 1 (294 responses)	School 2 (184 responses)
		%	%
– using hidden notes in written examination?	Yes	96.9	96.2
	No	1.7	2.7
	Unsure	1.4	1.1
– borrowing and copying another student's coursework with permission?	Yes	39.3	68.3
	No	42.4	20.8
	Unsure	18.3	10.9
– invention of laboratory data for experimental practicals?	Yes	40.0	65.9
	No	36.6	19.8
	Unsure	23.4	14.3

Source: Aggarwal, Bates, Davies, Khan: 'A study of academic dishonesty among students at two pharmacy schools.' Pharmaceutical Journal vol. 269, 12 October 2002, pp. 529–32.

The study also showed that students can clearly distinguish between degrees of impropriety, but it highlighted much uncertainty in particular scenarios. Only a minority of the students, for example, thought that 'borrowing another student's coursework for ideas for own work' would be problematic. Meanwhile, borrowing written material to stimulate one's own thinking, or verbal discussion with peers, is surely a major goal of a university education – provided it is acknowledged.

When the Plagiarism Advisory Service (PAS) was set up in 2003, plagiarism was generally believed to be widespread and deliberate. A study of 119 universities by the *Times Higher Education Supplement* in 2006 found that one in six students admitted cheating and more than a third used the Internet to plagiarise essays.[17] Now, a substantial 'cause' of cheating is believed to be simple ignorance about the importance of referencing data sources or how to do so. In a survey of more than 3,000 students conducted by the PAS at Northumbria University, 17 per cent of students were not confident that they could correctly incorporate the work of others into their own while staying within their university's rules. Only a third of students had had specifically taught sessions on study skills and best academic practice.[18]

The examination board Edexcel is to start using the US-designed detection program, Turnitin. All suspect scripts submitted to it, from GCSE level upwards, will be subject to customised 'originality reports', scanning the Internet for sites of origin of plagiarised material. Others believe that it is staff, not software, who will detect cheats in the war on plagiarism.[19] Staff, however, are confused by the wide range of penalties in use against plagiarists. The latest evidence from the PAS, in June 2007, suggests that a total of 25 different penalties are available for the offence across the sector, ranging from 'no further action' to expulsion. On the other hand, almost a third of higher education institutions, in their guidelines on plagiarism, fail to offer academic staff any guidance on which punishments are appropriate for different cases.[20] Baroness Deech, the student complaints ombudsman, has argued that the variation in penalties for plagiarism across the sector is 'too great to be defensible', and might not stand up to legal scrutiny. She said: 'The mere fact that this research has been carried out will alert all universities to the need to be fair and equitable in the way that they handle these offences and how they punish them... What is very good to see is that most universities are now tailoring the punishment to the offence.'[21] Universities are trying, but they're not there yet. However, of the student complaints to the ombudsman's office, only 2.8 per cent of complaints are about consistency and fairness in handling plagiarism allegations.[22]

All whose own work?

Researchers from the University of Central England have highlighted a new form of student plagiarism. They found that students were putting their coursework assignments out to tender online, with suppliers bidding to undertake the work. One in ten of all requests to one software outsourcing website were from students from 46 universities, suggesting that the problem is quite diffuse.[23]

However, there are some who argue for a change of attitude and a recognition of the positive benefits of providing model essays on the Internet. Peter Taylor of Acumen Professional Intelligence, a company whose websites, such as www.academicdb.com, provide access to '15,889 UK university essays and pieces of coursework written by students from virtually all disciplines', told an international conference for anti-plagiarism experts in 2006:

> There is very much an academic relevance in offering essays as examples of learning. This has a real academic use. Students can learn quickly from the best ideas of previous students. The biggest problem that our users face is the demonising of what we offer. When students are told that an essay site is a bad resource, they are not going to cite it properly. If there is a change of view in the academic community, it will encourage users to cite the work properly.[24]

In October 2006 the *Times Higher Education Supplement* (*THES*) reported on the stance of Dr Sean McGeogh, a part-time lecturer at Coventry University, and the company with which he is involved, Independent College and University Tutors (ICUT). The company was 'condemned by vice-chancellors as an "inappropriate" and "exploitative" business that could land students in trouble for cheating'. ICUT provides private tuition and proofreading services, but also, says its website, 'advice on improving essay content and presentation, so as to raise grades'. Dr McGeogh told *THES* that the service was 'a legitimate response to the poor-quality teaching offered by overcrowded and underfunded universities'. However, he added: 'I'm not happy that there is a gap in the market for organisations such as ICUT. Everything that they provide should be provided by the university system. But as one who works in the sector, I know all too well that there is no money to offer the kind of remedial courses and individual tutorial support that today's students vitally need... I know the failings of the university system, and I'm doing something constructive rather than just moaning.'[25]

Whose degree is it?

This insight into teachers', and students', dilemmas gives a second sense to the title of this book: who has earned this degree? The world of academe still retains unique pleasures and is not infrequently a privilege, for both staff and students. We owe a duty to our society to ensure that universities re-engage with their respected roles in teaching, research and broader social function. Our vocation is not in doubt, but there is a malignant cancer within the business of higher education. If these urgent issues are not quickly and satisfactorily addressed, the practical purpose of higher education will be lost.

Chapter 7

How Degrees are Awarded

How Degrees are Awarded

THE RANKING of undergraduate degrees as a First, Upper Second, Lower Second, Third or Pass provides a good example of how an apparently innocuous piece of academic theatre can have important implications:

- Some employers may not even invite for interview a graduate with a lower classification of degree.

- The pay that a graduate receives may be directly related to his or her degree classification.

- Some league tables use the number of Firsts and Upper Seconds as a measure of a university's success.

These facts have crucial importance for undergraduate students. So the vital questions are: how are the degree classifications decided, and are they reliable, meaningful and helpful?

First class or second class?

Ostensibly, the boundaries for degree rankings are:

- First: average marks over 70

- Upper Second (2:1): average marks 60–69

- Lower Second (2:2): average marks 50–59

- Third: average marks 40–49

- Pass: average lower than 40.

That is the theory. The reality is that boards of examiners, and the external examiners who consider the final examination marks, are academics who are supportive and sympathetic to their students. They retain a certain flexibility and common sense whilst attempting to maintain standards, and every year board decisions are usually focused on a protracted agony of indecision over the hapless candidates on the borderlines.

Is that an Upper Second or a teetering First?

Consider the following results for 18 hypothetical students (in reality the total list may include over 200 students). The final examination mark would be a composite mark from a number of examinations.

Table 7.1 Final year examination marks

	Final mark	Degree classification
Student 1	91.0	1
Student 2	71.0	1
Student 3	69.6	1 / 2.1?
Student 4	69.0	1 / 2.1?
Student 5	68.5	1 / 2.1?
Student 6	67.0	2.1
Student 7	64.3	2.1
Student 8	62.1	2.1
Student 9	60.3	2.1
Student 10	58.9	2.1 / 2.2?
Student 11	58.0	2.1 / 2.2?
Student 12	56.2	2.2
Student 13	55.5	2.2
Student 14	50.1	2.2
Student 15	48.9	2.2 / 3?
Student 16	48.6	2.2 / 3?
Student 17	42.6	3
Student 18	40.0	3

Who gets what? Students 1 and 2 are clear Firsts. But students 3 and 4 and possibly student 5 are very close to 70 and at many boards of examiners' meetings these students may be considered for a First. The examiners might also reflect that to award only two Firsts is perhaps considerably lower than in previous years and that this may have arisen due to slightly harder examination papers. Also, it may influence the examiners' judgement that awarding only two first-class honours this year may affect rankings in university league tables – a regrettable but real consideration. The examiners might also have been made aware that a student on the borderline may also have had difficult personal circumstances, such as health or financial problems, which may have adversely affected actual exam performance. The final number of first-class degrees awarded will depend on all these considerations, and precisely the same comments would apply to students on the other borderlines.

Now let's take things one step further. Final examination marks may be a composite from written examinations, laboratory coursework, presentations and other forms of assessment. Marks may be easier to achieve from, for example, coursework than from a written examination, so altering the proportion of marks awarded from these various sources affects the final mark. Such factors will vary between schools or departments within a university, and changes to the proportions may be entirely justified. But they also provide a way of manipulating the results, to ensure, for instance, that all students obtain a degree. This way lies grade inflation, intentional or unintentional.

Ranking students by their academic ability, which is the purpose of the degree classification, holds an implied assumption that all students have an equal chance of demonstrating their full academic potential. But some 25 per cent of students now live at home, which may incur two or three hours of travelling daily. Some students have to work many hours a week to survive financially. Clearly, not all students have an equal opportunity of demonstrating their full potential. To my knowledge, no board of examiners has even begun to approach this very real problem. It becomes difficult to believe that degree classification rankings are a reliable expression of academic ability even within a given department or course.

A matter of honour

In October 2001 reporter Patrick Healy revealed in the *Boston Globe* that Harvard University had a grade inflation culture that allowed 91 per cent of students to graduate with honours, rendering the distinction virtually meaningless. (At Yale the figure is about 51 per cent and at Princeton 44 per cent.)

Professor Harvey C. Mansfield, William R. Kennan Professor of Government, described as an outspoken critic of political correctness and of declining standards on campus, and Harvard's resident gadfly on the subject of grade inflation, said he tried to reclaim his 'own integrity' by giving Cs and even Ds for work that deserved it. On the first day of class he told students he would give them two grades: one 'official' mark – usually an A or B pumped up by Harvard's inflationary trend – and a second grade that reflected the actual quality of their work and effort. When Professor Mansfield made public the results of his two-grade policy, as well as his students' anonymous evaluations of him, he provided a glimpse into one Harvard classroom that was openly dealing with grade inflation.

Harvard has no single grading scale, and Mansfield could give lower grades if he wanted, as some professors do. But he says this would unfairly penalise his students who compete against classmates for honours and places in graduate school. Mansfield said he wanted to hold his colleagues and administration up to ridicule. But he also hoped to embarrass them into taking collective action to make grading more rigorous.

The ensuing furore (see graphics.boston.com/globe/metro/packages/harvard_honors) makes hilarious reading but also raises some worrying questions. That Harvard could be reducing its standards was a breathtaking indictment and one from which universities in the UK are not immune.

A lucky dip with a lifetime of consequences

To suggest that an examination system can mark to an accuracy of within 1 or 2 per cent is questionable, and to suggest that a candidate who gains a mark of 71 is academically so superior to a candidate with a mark of 68.5 as to be placed in a separate class is as absurd as the distinction is artificial. Similarly, to suggest that the candidate who obtains an outstanding mark of 91 is placed in the same category as one with a mark of 71, or that a student with a mark of 60.3 may obtain the same class of degree as a student with a mark of 69 is again seriously misleading about the academic achievement. It is not surprising that Peter Williams, Chief Executive of the Quality Assurance Agency (QAA) and a member of the Measuring and Recording Student Achievement Group (see below), has said that the traditional system 'is much too rough and ready... there are no nationally agreed methods for ensuring consistency and no common descriptions of what each class represents. So for students, it is a bit of a lucky dip with a lifetime of consequences.'[1]

But there are also clear differences in degree class awarded by departments within a university. The QAA questioned the fairness of assessment practices at Sheffield University after discovering that it uses two different systems to classify students' final degrees and that there is variation between departments in the rules that allow students to progress from the first to the second year. This occurred because the university could not reconcile differing but deeply held views within its academic community. A lucky dip indeed. It is most unlikely that this scenario is to be found only in Sheffield University.

Which of our brightest students get a First is now described as a lottery based on the choice of course and university. In October 2006 the Higher Education Policy Institute (HEPI) reported many cases of disparity between the proportion of good degrees awarded and the 'cleverness' of the student on entry. For example, graduates of media studies at Sunderland are more likely to leave with Firsts and Upper Seconds than those reading maths at Birmingham. Warwick awards more good degrees for history and philosophy than Oxford or Cambridge and Bath gives out more Firsts and Upper Seconds for biological science than Nottingham.[2]

There also appears to be a mismatch relating to degree class output and the hours devoted to study. Six-in-ten students of physical sciences at Plymouth, who came in with average A level grades of CCD and worked an average 20 hours a week, graduated with a First or 2.1. The same proportion gained top degrees at Birmingham having average A-level grades of AAB and having worked a 26.4 hour week.[3]

Bahram Bekhradnia, the director of the HEPI, said he was sending its findings to Universities UK, which is conducting an inquiry into the system of degree classification. He commented: 'We have raised the question of how it is that some universities seem to provide a higher proportion of firsts and 2.1s when they don't have a high proportion of clever students and they don't seem to work very hard.'[4]

Lukewarm reception for change

The HEPI report complemented the verdict of a QAA briefing paper on the system for awarding student degree classifications. The QAA paper supported accusations that degree classifications are unsafe, indicating that is not possible to compare the performance of students at different universities and that frequently there is little point in comparing degree results from the same university: 'It cannot be assumed that students graduating with the same classified degree from a particular institution, having studied different subjects, will have achieved similar academic standards.' Thus joint-honours students were 'significantly less likely to achieve a first-class degree than those studying a single subject'.[5]

The QAA paper was prepared for the Burgess Group (more formally known as the Measuring and Recording Student Achievement Group), led by Leicester University vice-chancellor Bob Burgess. The group, whose enquiries were prompted by the 2003 White Paper *The future of higher education*, is consulting on plans to abolish the traditional classification system, on the grounds that it is 'not fit for purpose' and 'can mislead rather than inform'.[6]

In September 2005 the group published proposals for a simple pass/fail system with a 'distinction' reserved for an elite. This would be accompanied by a detailed transcript of a student's achievement across all individual elements of their degree. It had to acknowledge, however, that there was insufficient support for its plans. Only about half of respondents 'indicated a measure of agreement with the need to replace the UK classification system', and the specific pass/fail/distinction plan 'did not find favour'.[7] The following represent some of the specific responses.

- Peter Williams, chief executive of the QAA, said: 'Whatever proposals emerge in the coming months must be meaningful, easy to understand and have the confidence of the public.'

- Universities UK, which represents vice-chancellors, said the variation in distribution of degree classification raised 'some interesting questions'.

- The Association of Graduate Recruiters suggested that there should be a five-year moratorium on any change to classifications, warning that employers preferred 'the devil they know'.

- The Institute of Directors and the University and College Union considered that the outcome would be too crude.

- The head of the Association of Heads of University Administration said that while the AHUA had not taken a collective view, he personally did not support the plan for a pass/fail system: 'The system of classified honours degrees is massively ingrained in the psyches of employers, graduates and students. It would be much less perilous to reform than abandon it.'[8]

What is the conclusion?

Higher education does not have a primary moral or legal obligation to arrange its credentialing to the satisfaction of graduate recruiters, employers or the public. But four years after the problem was clearly identified in the White Paper on higher education it is surely time to demonstrate its professional responsibilities and honour its moral and ethical responsibilities to its students and lead by example.

Employers, whilst accepting that there is a real problem with degree classifications, do not support their demise. They do not want to sift through detailed academic information. They would prefer to make it harder for students to attain 2:1s and Firsts. However, employers should welcome transcripts because, apart from giving a more exact indication than a grade, they would indicate in which parts of the curriculum the student performed better and this may be relevant to the particular career opportunities on offer (see Chapter 11).

'Everyone seems to agree that the classification system is outdated,' said Wes Streeting, vice-president of the National Union of Students and a member of the Burgess Group. 'But, as ever, there is no consensus about what should replace it. We can't allow the sector to resort to the status quo because it is not brave enough.'[9]

The reader may remain perplexed that many UK universities so needlessly complicate a student's record of achievement. It would be a nonsense to pretend that a single mark or marks reflect a robust difference in academic or indeed any other ability. Yet that is the consequence of using degree classifications and seductive rankings. For the record, UK medical and veterinary schools simply award the original examination marks and provide their students with a transcript of the actual marks obtained – like most universities in every country in the world.

Chapter 8

The Rights of Students ... or Lack of Them

The Rights of Students... or Lack of Them

A DISTINGUISHING FEATURE OF a university is that it is a 'community of scholars', the teachers and their students engaged in the search for truth. The community is distinguished in turn by the gift of 'academic freedom', enshrined in the UK Education Reform Act of 1998 (section 202(2)) as:

> Freedom within the law to question and test received
> wisdom and to put forward new ideas and controversial and
> unpopular opinions, without placing themselves in jeopardy
> of losing their jobs.

Such freedom is vigorously defended and considered to extend to the student body, since both staff and students undertake intellectual and independent enquiry.[1] However, the relationship between the university and its academic staff is fundamentally different from the relationship between the university and its students. There is an employer–employee relationship between university and staff which carries a clear-cut duty of care and a conduct of behaviour for both parties. Neither should embarrass the reputation of the other. But if things do go wrong, the staff and university are entitled to remedies within the law, as employees and employer.

But the student is not an employee of the university, more a client or customer, and this has resulted in most unfortunate consequences for many students. If a student buys clothes or books a holiday, and the goods or service turn out to be below standard, and if polite negotiation to remedy the situation does not succeed, as an adult (i.e. a person aged over 18 years) the student, like anyone else in our society, can seek a remedy through the courts.

However, as a student, if the course for which he or she registered at university is clearly not as described in the prospectus, or the quality of teaching falls below fair and reasonable standards, it may prove very difficult to seek redress through the legal system. In brief, the student may effectively be denied reasonable access to the courts. This appears unjust. For, 'If doctors, lawyers, architects, engineers, and other professionals are charged with a duty owing to the public whom they serve, it could not be said that nothing in the law precludes similar treatment of professional educators.'[2]

For students, accountability in higher education remains a conundrum. Whilst standards are set and expected for themselves and for the curriculum, a student disadvantaged by inadequate education may have serious problems in seeking redress. How has this most unfortunate situation arisen?

A student may believe that it is 'only fair' that they should receive compensation for a substantial loss of teaching and potential damage to career prospects. And they would find support in the views of Sir Geoffrey Holland, former vice-chancellor of Exeter University and a past permanent secretary at the Department of Education who advocates a guarantee to students of refunds for unsatisfactory items in a course.[3] However, the bad news for the student is that they may fail to obtain compensation. Furthermore, some academic staff actually believe that students should not be entitled to compensation. An editorial in the *Times Higher Education Supplement* was firm on the subject:

> Students who pay the full cost of their education – even on credit – may think they have the same right to complain about the service as anyone else spending money. But it does not do students any favours for Sir Geoffrey Holland to suggest that they deserve a refund if their experience fails to live up to their expectations... students become partners in an experience in which they are full participants and where – one hopes – no cheque will buy a degree unless the exams have been passed. Students go to university in part to learn to think for themselves and to gain intellectual self-confidence. Telling them that they can get their money back if it goes wrong sends the message that they are there, instead, as passive recipients of a product. It would be more honest to say that going to university is a right for all those who can gain from the experience but that making the most of it is as much their responsibility as the university's.[4]

Some academic staff may feel uncomfortable at the obfuscation in this editorial. The issue is not about experiences which 'fail to live up to expectations'. It is about sub-standard care.

This chapter is about the unusual legal relationship that a student has with his or her university, the internal university procedures and the external legal frameworks that exist (or in some cases don't exist) between the student and university to correct situations when things go wrong. It should also help in an understanding of the deep inadequacies in the present system to protect students and help to prevent the occurrence of misunderstandings. Clear expectations of the student will in turn also improve procedures, the standards of provision and the smooth running of universities. They will also reduce compensation claims.

What is the nature of a university–student relationship?

The traditional universities have been autonomous institutions that determined the nature and purpose of their work, set their own standards and effectively answered only to themselves. They are fiercely protective of this independence which has enabled higher education to resist interference by the state. But by the same token, it makes it difficult to hold universities to account if they do not behave responsibly with staff or students.

However, one of the uses of an earned degree is to inform others of the holder's knowledge and skills – employers want to know what their applicants are capable of – and in the public perception this develops universities from being just a 'community of scholars' to being 'quality service providers'. Within this perspective it is easy to see students as 'purchasers', 'customers' or 'consumers'. If this is correct, then university teachers are professionals who, like all professionals, must maintain high professional standards, and be held accountable for their actions.

Two models have been advanced to attempt to define the university–student relationship, albeit with differing degrees of success.

The 'commercial' model

In higher education the focus on accountability, efficiency and value for money has mesmerised many administrators into considering the university–student relationship as a commercial enterprise in a free market. The university is a 'factory', the academics are the 'workers', and the student is a 'customer' who requests to be transformed into a product called a 'graduate', finally stamped either fit for purpose with a degree, or rejected as substandard. In brief, providing we can view a human being as comparable to a sausage, car, or a package of detergent, our finished product, a graduate, is simply the expression of a manufacturing process. And providing we can conclude that the quality of the product is entirely an expression of the higher educational process, we might be able to partially sustain an argument. Apart from three problems.

First, the 'customer' or 'product' was well formed even before he or she entered the educational process – unlike a sausage. Secondly, whilst within higher education the product is continually exposed to both known and unknown external influences that can dramatically affect the quality of the finished product. Thirdly, no matter how skilled the workers, and no matter how efficient the production line, the product itself has to actively partake in and contribute to the development of its own quality. To obtain meaningful benefit from a university education the student must develop a maximal involvement with the production/educational process. This is not guaranteed, and final success is critically dependent on the committed involvement of the student. For this reason, to my knowledge, no university anywhere in the world has been able to guarantee its 'product'. Also, unlike the purchase of a normal product, universities do not 'do refunds' – unless breach of contract or negligence rear their ugly heads.

A further difficulty with this model is that, after taking the student's money, the responsibility of the university may not finally be to the student but to society. Society as a stakeholder in education requires, for example, that doctors, nurses and pharmacists achieve a satisfactory level of competence to avoid future harm to their patients; that engineers have the knowledge and skills to make sure that the bridges they build do not fall down.

There also remains the most important criticism that appears to have escaped the corporate mindset when thinking of a graduate as a customer. If you ask undergraduate students or graduates if they wish to be considered as a customer, let alone a sausage, you invariably receive a brisk response: absolutely not. Most detest the idea. So, surely, we can do better than this contrived nonsense.

Yes, the students do purchase a service. But they also want to be actively involved and be seen to be involved in their own education and, most important, to be given full credit for their determined application and success. For most people, obtaining a degree remains one of the greatest milestones in life.

The 'medical' model

A better model may be found in the doctor–patient relationship (excepting, thankfully, that most of our students remain in robust good health). The goal of both healthcare and education is to improve the condition of their clients. But both have an important qualifying caution: the success of healthcare and education is critically related to the active cooperation of the patient or student. A patient that ignores sound medical advice or fails to take medication, or a student that does not give of his or her best under the tutor's guidance, contributes to their own downfall. And quite reasonably, neither healthcare nor education wish to be held accountable for such failures.

But this raises a profound challenge. How do we distinguish the proportionate contribution made by the student from that of the college or university? Does the student contribute 90 per cent or 10 per cent to his or her final academic success, or somewhere in between? No one knows – but we do know that it will vary between students.

The reality is that, for most universities and academic staff, students arrive, are taught and then graduate. Most institutions and staff have little if any knowledge, interest or more importantly time to formally assess the nature of the success or failure of the interaction between student, staff and institution. The interaction between university and student has generally been assumed to have had merit; the degree of merit has remained essentially unknown.

This is unsettling. Students appear to pay many thousands of pounds to enter an educational process the benefit of which is uncertain. And measuring student 'failures' or 'successes' in higher education on the basis of a simple exam mark, as frequently occurs, is beset with problems. Professor Astin, a psychologist and the Allan M. Cartter Professor of Education at the University of California, Los Angeles, has developed a comparison between the patient–healthcare relationship and that which exists between a student and education. To paraphrase: patients or students seeking advice or tuition are admitted to hospitals or universities/colleges. It is inevitable that the outcome of the intervention will vary between patients and students. Some patients improve and some students learn even if the intervention is ineffectual. In the presence of a poor prognosis a modest outcome may be judged highly successful for the patient or student. Conversely, the intervention could be judged a failure if a patient or student with a favourable prognosis fails to improve after treatment. In any event, patient or student compliance with the treatment or education remains unknown. In brief, the purported success or failure of the intervention has meaning only in the context of the initial prognosis and compliance to the advice or tuition.[5]

Students have a legal relationship with a university, but not with the teachers, with whom they have a far more important relationship. To continue with Professor Astin's analogy, the interaction is of a professional exercising their superior knowledge and skills to the best of their ability. Accountants, lawyers, engineers and many others also exercise such professional skills in the best interests of their clients. Just as a patient may perhaps be considered a client, so too might a student similarly metamorphose into a client. And within the unequal encounter of an experienced academic and a student or 'client', the essential basis of a professional–client relationship is, as always, one of trust and integrity. This raises substantial ethical issues when, as we shall see, institutional practice is at odds with this professional–client relationship.

The contract

So, how do the two parties in higher education formalise their relationship? A contract is a bargain between two parties and is based on trust and mutual obligations. Both the university and student (and the staff) are expected not to behave in a manner that may damage the relationship of trust. Both agree to certain undertakings and the contract continues as long as both parties honour their agreements. For a student, the contract is secured when the university makes an 'offer' (it may initially be conditional on certain A-level grades or points) and the student 'accepts'. The acceptance by the student of a place at a university will then include paying fees and agreeing to the rules of the university. The defining moment is when the student enrols or registers.

The university agrees:

- to admit the student and allow him or her to attend the specified and promised course;

- to provide the student with satisfactory teaching and adequate facilities;

- to examine the student to fulfil the requirements so that he or she can obtain a qualification.

The university may make changes to the courses if the prospectus says that the university reserves this right. Success in the relationship is irretrievably linked to high standards of teaching and learning by both the university and the student, but the relationship has never been really equal. The university has, after all, made its own terms and, in the final analysis, the student can either take it or leave it.

Inequality between universities

A fundamental difficulty is that, although all students have contracts with their universities, not all students share the same rights and responsibilities. This may be important if the student wishes to voice a concern or make a complaint. The following is an attempt to simplify a complex situation by placing universities into three groups.

Group 1: Pre-1992 universities

If a student joins a university that was established before 1992, that is, a 'chartered university', the student becomes a 'corporator' or 'member'. The membership derives from 'incorporation': a student is made a 'member' of a 'body' called a university. This is derived from the ancient tradition that a university is a guild to which its members, that is, the scholars, belong for life. The major consequence for the student is that membership requires them to obey the 'domestic laws' of the university. In being 'domestic' a university is rather like a club and this carries very important legal connotations. Even if it is accepted that there has been a procedural error, an injustice, or that something has gone wrong, and it was clearly the university's fault, the courts are reluctant to intervene in the private affairs of a 'domestic' forum, even when they would normally take an interest in, for example, breach of contract.

For example, in the resolution of a complaint by a student, the student would have to proceed first through all the internal procedures of the university. This usually terminates in processing the complaint through the so-called 'university visitor'. Only when all the internal procedures have been exhausted and a remedy has not been found, it *may* be possible to go to external or judicial review.

Group 2: Oxford and Cambridge

Oxford and Cambridge universities are 'civil corporations', and a similar situation exists, where a Proctor adjudicates.

Group 3: Post-1992 new universities

These are 'statutory corporations', indicating that the new universities have been set up under statutes and they do not have 'visitors' like the older chartered universities. However, like their older sisters they do have internal mechanisms to consider complaints. In the absence of a 'visitor', it is likely that the courts will allow students from the new universities to apply for public law remedies and leave for judicial review. It has more recently come to be held that new universities, and perhaps Oxford and Cambridge, have 'the ordinary attributes of legal personality and a capacity to enter into contracts'.[6] It may be argued that they are also public bodies, and this raises questions whether a litigant should seek a public law route, such as judicial review, rather than to sue in contract.[7]

It is manifestly unfair that students in all universities do not have the same rights and remedies in the courts, and where so many continue to be subject to the jurisdiction of the university visitor. In their book on education law Evans and Gill state: 'It cannot be overemphasised that, this is an immensely difficult problem for the student who cannot, in effect, get "outside" the domestic forum of his university for an independent decision about his complaint.'[8] Gillian Evans has extensive experience both in teaching in higher education and in case law. Jaswinder Gill is a leading lawyer and expert in educational law, advising students on the protection of rights.

It is vitally important that a student receives expert advice when trying to establish whether a complaint falls within the realm of private law (that is, where there is a legally binding relationship, such as contract, between the two parties) or public law, such as judicial review (where the overarching consideration is whether a public duty has been ignored). The student must also be aware that there are statutory time factors for putting claims to the courts. Only three months are allowed for seeking judicial review; a claim for personal injury must be submitted within three years; a claim arising out of contract or negligence must be brought within six years. So, if the student is delayed in the internal procedures of his or her university, this may seriously compromise the opportunity of accessing the court.[9]

Evans and Gill advise students:

> If you need legal advice try the students' union first so as to get free legal advice in that way if you can. Alternatively, if, like most students, you have a low income, you will

be entitled to up to two hours' free advice and assistance under the 'legal help at court' scheme provided by the Legal Services Commission. If you are not eligible for that scheme, ask for a meeting with a solicitor. If you go to a solicitor check that you have approached one with specialist knowledge. Get the solicitor to try writing a warning letter or suggest alternative dispute resolution as a means of avoiding a court case.

Do not begin legal action unless you are prepared for a very long and stressful study.[10]

Universities have a clear obligation to provide adequate teaching and feedback, and to ensure that students can properly prepare for their examinations. But the courts have long questioned the concept of a 'duty of care' in education, so this inevitably remains a grey area when so much is subjective and accountability difficult to prove.

The nature of complaints

The Privy Council, which acts as visitor to 17 universities, noticed a huge increase in student complaints in 2003. Alex Galloway, Clerk to the Privy Council, says it now receives about 40 complaints a year, rather than the half-dozen or so of five years ago, although this increase has much to do with the Privy Council's higher profile in providing students with information and assistance. He has also instituted greater openness in the Council's deliberations on complaints, such as making the reason behind judgements available, but admits that limited time and resources mean that the visitor system provides only 'amateur justice, at least as operated in this office'.[11]

Subsequently, hundreds of complaints have been made about erroneous exam papers, inadequate facilities and cancelled classes, poor-quality accommodation, incompetent lecturers, obsolete facilities, the timing and quality of feedback for an assessment, staff shortages, timetable clashes and other contentious issues. At Edge Hill College, Merseyside, for example, 44 students complained that one lecturing venue was 'not appropriate as a lecture hall for 60 third-year students (poor acoustics, no note-taking facilities)'. It is disquieting to note, however, that, two-thirds of all students' complaints are not upheld.[12] Typical complaints raised by undergraduate students focus on the following areas.

Concerns related to facilities and resources

The lecture rooms are too small to accommodate all students, too cold to allow us to write, too large to allow us to hear the lecturer, too dispersed around the campus making us late for sequential lectures. The audio-visual facilities frequently fail; the photocopying facilities are either dysfunctional or overused; the number of computers is insufficient to student usage. Why is the library not open 24 hours a day as in other universities?

Concerns related to teaching and course organisation

It is not clear what I am expected to do. Students in some of my lectures appear to come from different courses with different levels of interest or commitment. Some students on my course are disruptive, spoiling the teaching experience, with the university failing to correct or remove the students. The course standards are questionable and appear inferior. Lectures are cancelled with little notice and are not re-scheduled. Some lectures are badly prepared with marked differences in the quality of presentation. The quality of staff supervision of student-centered learning is variable and we appear to be teaching ourselves; small-group seminars and tutorials are being reduced or displaced; we do not see much of senior academic staff but their postgraduate research students.

Concerns related to feedback on submitted work

Submitted work seems to be returned slowly with little if any written comments.

Concerns about examinations and assessments

When we are working on group projects where we are encouraged to use shared facilities and activities, plagiarism should be carefully defined. My mitigating circumstances of personal/medical/disability problems were not passed on to the examiners. I was not allowed any extra time for my special needs.

Altogether, students made 6,796 formal complaints and appeals in 2003. In 2004, the figure rose to 8,682. Around a third of complaints in a year are upheld and a total of more than £300,000 paid out in refunds and compensation.[13] Jan Harris, deputy head of the education student issues group with the law firm Eversheds, has noticed a sharp increase in complaints being referred to her firm and also sees that parents are becoming more vociferous: 'Parents are having to stump up more than they were, and there is a whole ethos of parents getting more involved... At least a third of complaints I deal with, I would say, have some form of direct or indirect parental involvement.' [14]

University complaints procedures: the theory and reality

Student complaints may result in mild annoyance or irritation, or may escalate to real bitterness and resentment, with subsequent legal proceedings. This may not be surprising when the normal university procedures for dealing with complaints, the procedures with which students have to begin, are seen in the following perspective. For many universities, it seems, have not taken student complaints very seriously.

Back in 1997 the report of Dearing's National Committee of Enquiry into Higher Education (www.leeds.ac.uk/educol/ncihe) acknowledged the urgent need for something to be done to improve the handling of complaints from students. Its Recommendation 60 said:

> We recommend to institutions that, over the next two years, they review and, if necessary, amend their arrangements for handling complaints from students, to ensure that they reflect the principles of natural justice; they are transparent and timely; they include procedures for reconciliation and arbitration; they include an independent external element; and they are managed by a senior member of staff.

The Government's response to Dearing, *Higher education for the twenty-first century*, reinforced the recommendations.

The Quality Assurance Agency's (QAA) guidelines published in 2000 reflected uncertainties relating to the Human Rights Act 1998 and the 'independent element' in the complaints procedures. The latter would have taken appeal or arbitration outside the universities but, being autonomous institutions, the universities need not consent to that. This is a crucial point for students, who may find that their complaints are delayed or not effectively addressed inside the institution, and who then require an external intervention, if it can still be achieved.

The National Union of Students recommendations

The NUS Good Practice Guides consider the student rights that universities must respect when complaints are made. They include the following:[15]

- a right to complain without fear of being subjected to a disciplinary action

- a right to act as a group where several complainants have the same complaint

- a right to information about the grounds on which complaints may be made, the procedures adopted and the time scale of events*

- a right to independent judgement (this is particularly important since, in its absence, the university is acting as accuser, jury, judge and executioner in its own case!)

- a right to representation

- a right to a fair hearing

- a right to an appropriate remedy (perhaps restoring the student to the position he or she was in before the problem began; awarding a degree; fulfilling the contractual obligations;** or seeking damages).

* For example: publication of clear step-by-step procedures; creating a culture that, wherever possible, problems will be resolved quickly and informally; informed help provided to the student to identify the grounds for complaint or appeal; disclosure of documents.

** The legal requirements inherent in the contract between student and university have to be honoured; there is also an implied contractual duty to treat the student fairly and not to breach the Unfair Terms in Consumer Contracts Regulations 1994. Public funding of universities also requires that they meet Public Law Standards of fairness.

The reality is unfortunately somewhat different from the ideals identified in the NUS Good Practice Guides (see box). In their final analysis with respect to complaints, disputes and appeals, Evans and Gill concluded that:

> ... anyone intimate with the running of universities and the ways in which they handle complaints and appeals and disputes with their students and staff would find it hard not to be aware that a great culture change is needed... for the individual student is in a weak and precarious position. Hundreds, perhaps thousands, of lives full of promise are being cut short professionally by incompetence in the administration of universities and colleges... The fault lies for the most part not in lack of goodwill, but in lack of training, expertise and sheer awareness of the obligation upon providers of higher education, and lack of funding to enable universities to put their house in order in this area.[16]

These eminent education lawyers say that the youth and lack of experience of most students emphasise the need for universities to help them to a fair hearing and redress without recourse to the law. They recognise universities' need for autonomy and independence, but ask for 'a degree of humility and common sense, a willingness to admit error and lapses of procedural fairness when they occur and goodwill to put things right for the sake of students whose futures are at stake'.[17]

Making complaints and the risk of reprisals

Most students are reluctant to complain, perceiving their vulnerable position. They have not yet been awarded their degrees and will be dependent on good references from the university. How will future employers view the value of a student's degree from a university where the student has questioned the standards of the university? The student is in a most unenviable position. Making complaints against other students may also invite overt or subtle retribution.

The law is of limited help in ensuring fair play. The Committee of Vice-Chancellors and Principals (CVCP) guidelines (1999) on the Public Interest Disclosure Act are intended to cover both students and staff: 'No detrimental action of any kind will be taken under this procedure against a person within the institution making a complaint of the nature described above, provided it is done without malice and in good faith, reasonably believing it to be true.'

However, can the student really speak without fear of reprisal? The CVCP guidelines may prevent formal disciplinary action, yet who amongst an academic (or any other) community has not witnessed subtle reprisals or bad-mouthing? Care when making complaints is vital.

Academic institutions, like other large organisations, have a knee-jerk reaction: complaints signal trouble and generate defensive postures. This delays problem solving, mediation and the re-establishment of friendly relations. It can also get much worse. If the student does not believe his or her complaint is being taken seriously to prevent future mishaps, then this may result (and has done so) in external activities involving the media. There are few winners in this scenario and universities detest the publicity. It is surely much better to avoid this by establishing in the first place the prudent care of students.

Universities will usually fight hard and ruthlessly against their own students once the matter reaches the courts. They have a great deal more money than the student and, if the student loses, the university may try to recover the enormous costs against the students. Universities dislike damage to their reputations. The media can be used as a 'pressure group' to encourage the university to settle with you but that should be a last resort because you will have no control over the way they tell the story.[18]

The future of the visitor

In March 2003 the High Court considered a complaint that had a particular bearing on the visitor system that pertains in all pre-1992 universities. In 1997 Mr Kevin Wilkinson left a well-paid teaching job in Dubai and relocated with his wife and two children to begin a PhD at Aston. But when he arrived he found that, despite assurances given before the move, there was no one properly qualified to supervise him; his agreed tutor had left the university. After a long dispute, the vice-chancellor of Aston, Michael Wright, agreed that Mr Wilkinson's experience had been 'far from satisfactory', offered him an apology and instigated a full refund of his fees. But the now Dr Wilkinson, having meanwhile gained his PhD at another university, believed he was entitled to large damages for the wasted time and loss of potential earnings. He refused to refer his complaint to Aston's visitor and, represented by the education lawyer Jaswinder Gill, argued in the High Court in 2003 that the visitor system was outdated, lacked independence and sufficient expertise, and was not capable of supplying Dr Wilkinson with the kind of remedy he required. It was hoped to set a legal precedent by asking the High Court to override the visitor's jurisdiction.[19]

The attempt failed. His bid for damages was struck out in its entirety on the grounds that the claim fell within the exclusive jurisdiction of the quasi-judicial visitor, who, according to precedent, has exclusive jurisdiction over student complaints. The visitor in Aston's case is the Queen.

However, in May that year leading human rights lawyer Cherie Booth QC argued that the decision had been wrong. Citing Article 6 of the Human Rights Act, which ensures 'right of access to court', Ms Booth said: 'The visitor system was not a tribunal that complied with Article 6, and therefore the existence of a right of appeal to the visitor does not itself satisfy the right of access to court.' She went on: 'A hearing before a visitor is not compliant with Article 6, in that there is no right to an oral hearing, and it is not in public... nor is it before an independent tribunal, nor are there any rules regarding the appointment of visitors or the procedure which they must follow.' She also argued that the decision to throw out Dr Wilkinson's application for damages was a breach of Article 14 of the convention, which prohibits discrimination on the grounds of a person's 'status'. Non-members of the university could take it to court, but if the master's judgement was upheld, then any person who became a member of the university would be prevented from turning to the courts: 'Thus there is a difference in treatment over access to the courts between members of the university and all others seeking to enforce contractual remedies.'[20]

The case was watched closely by legal experts who have long suspected that the visitor system is in breach of human rights legislation. But there has not been a test case to fully challenge the exclusive jurisdiction. Will the Office of the Independent Adjudicator (OIA), more widely known as the Student Ombudsman, herald a new beginning in student access to justice?

The Student Ombudsman

The first independent adjudicator, announced in October 2003, was Ruth Deech, principal of St Anne's College, Oxford. Baroness Warwick, Chief Executive of Universities UK, speaking at a 'students' complaints' conference, said students have every right to call their universities to account. 'Long gone are the times when it was considered that the recipients of higher education were privileged and should be grateful for whatever they received. Today's students quite rightly have high expectations.' Welcoming the establishment of the Office of the Independent Adjudicator for Higher Education in England and Wales, she said: 'We should see this development as a supplement to, not a substitution for, our internal procedures.'[21] Jaswinder Gill was perhaps less impressed, saying: 'What students want are transparent procedures that take account of the fact that every day's delay damages a student's education and yet means nothing to the university.'[22]

The OIA opened in March 2004 and was immediately challenged with being in breach of human rights law. A key concern is that it is unlikely to conform to Article 6 of the European Convention on Human Rights, which guarantees the right to a fair and public hearing. Tim Birtwistle, a law professor at Leeds Metropolitan University who has advised the European Network of Higher Education Ombudsmen, said: 'I am at a loss to understand this wasted opportunity. Article 6 of the Human Rights Convention enshrines the right to a fair hearing, and this was a key criticism of the old system. How can both sides put their arguments if this is going to be just another paper exercise? And there is the question of unequal arms, with universities wheeling out their team of experts'.

Students must complain to the visitor, who may seek advice from the OIA. The OIA will provide 'a letter of advice' to the visitor, 'who will then issue his or her decision', the OIA says. 'There is no appeal to us from the visitor's decision and the OIA's advice letter will not be sent to students.'[23]

Several universities have already decided not to opt into the scheme while it remains voluntary. The higher education bill is expected to put the OIA on a legal footing. But until then it is hard to disagree with the conclusions drawn by Dr Wilkinson's, wife: 'This independent adjudicator is a sham while the visitor is in place.'[24]

But for Dr Wilkinson, his wife and future students there may be a happy ending. Dr Wilkinson, backed by Cherie Booth QC, finally reached a settlement with Aston University over his dispute, and the visitor's jurisdiction was finally declared unlawful under human rights laws.[25]

Students stand up for their rights

Government officials and student leaders welcomed the increase in complaints from students as a sign that those paying tuition fees were standing up for their rights. A spokesman for the Department for Education and Skills said: 'It is right that students have high expectations of the institution that they attend.'

A spokesperson for Universities UK claimed that institutions 'have established procedures for dealing with student complaints and make these procedures known to all students'. Kat Fletcher, the president of the National Union of Students, remarked that, 'With a funding system that increasingly views a degree as a commodity, it is hardly surprising that students are starting to view themselves as consumers.'[26] Academic staff who are condemned to give lectures in rooms inadequate to the purpose of teaching will also be hopeful that the university will be pressurised to improve facilities. Matt Waddup, assistant general secretary for the Association of University Teachers, said that students were bound to encounter genuine problems as a result of poor levels of funding and a plethora of red tape. 'Our members report that with ever more external regulation and assessment of their research and teaching, as well as increasing demands on administrative staff, they have less and less time to spend with students,' he said. 'Student-to-staff ratios are now higher in universities than in schools, and this will inevitably have an impact. As most students would agree, university staff continue to do an amazing job in increasingly difficult circumstances.'[27]

As we have noted above, however, approximately 70 per cent of the claims were not upheld. These may reflect a rise in vexatious complaints. The lecturers' union Natfhe had warned that an unwelcome 'commodification' of higher education was leading to a complaints culture that was diverting time and resources away from teaching and research, while putting intolerable pressure on lecturers faced with often spurious allegations.[28]

Dame Ruth, the independent adjudicator, claimed that the upward trend was explained in part by rising student numbers. In addition, she added, the increasingly crowded graduate jobs market meant that there was greater pressure on students to succeed. She also suggested that the effort to attract more students from working-class backgrounds, while an entirely legitimate goal, contributed to the rise in the number of complaints. Non-traditional and overseas students were more likely to encounter problems with support and language and to experience culture clashes. The introduction of tuition fees is a crucial factor. 'The more people feel they're paying, the more they feel they are entitled to examine what they're getting for their money… Once parents become conscious of paying a lot, they'll be much more insistent on getting what they pay for,' she said. The end of free education had changed the student culture: 'Regrettably, students see themselves as consumers rather than participants in a process. Higher education is not a consumer product, but a participatory product,' she said.[29]

Perhaps the editorial in the *Times Higher Education Supplement* in August 2005 summarised the new complaints situation best:

> The new culture is bound to breed resentment among academics and administrators, who perceive the system as weighted in favour of students. The natural caution that this encourages can sour relationships and work against students in the long run. But higher education was never going to be immune from the trend towards litigation that pervades other walks of life. Like it or not, universities and colleges will have to get used to it. They have not always provided good service in the past and, until recently, have not made it easy for aggrieved students to secure justice. The challenge will be to ensure that the balance does not swing so far that the collegial basis of student and academic life is lost.[30]

For some universities, humility and common sense were not apparent in July 2007. Senior university administrators were reported to be preparing for the use of a legal contract that would actually restrict even further student rights to seek compensation if, for example, a course was not run or was changed, or if promises made were not upheld. The NUS has attacked it as one-sided, emphasising that education is not a commodity but a partnership. Sally Hunt, general secretary of the University and College Union, said: 'The shift towards a market in higher education is inevitably bringing about a consumer culture. The biggest losers so far have been students and staff. But vice-chancellors must also be prepared to reap what they sow. If students are unhappy with the service provided they are much more likely to seek redress.'[31]

Mediation instead of confrontation

But there is another way of approaching conflicts, although it would require a major cultural change in higher education. According to the Oxford Centre for Higher Education Policy Studies, universities spend an average of £100,000 a year on legal fees, most of which goes on defending legal claims against students and staff. Settlement costs can reach six-figure sums. A two-year project, which is called Transforming Policy and Practice in Dispute Resolution in HEIs, funded by the Higher Education Funding Council for England, will investigate 'mediation' as a way of avoiding big legal costs and years of stress and wasted management time. Unlike arbitration, a mediator does not have the authority to arrive at a decision. Instead, the mediator's job is to find a solution that both parties can agree on.

Doug Yarn, professor of law at Georgia State University, offers a US perspective on the project. He said:

> As in all organisations, conflict in institutions of higher education is inevitable... In contrast to adjudication, mediation works through consensus. In the 35 colleges and universities that comprise the University System of Georgia, we have been using it effectively to reduce the costs of conflict in disputes ranging from roommate spats to employment discrimination to revolts by faculty against department heads and college presidents. We have prevented costly lawsuits and improved internal relationships and modes of decision-making.[32]

It will be of interest to see whether mediation can alter the UK culture of student complaints and how they are viewed. Details of OxCHEPS Higher Education Mediation Service are found at http//oxcheps.new.ox.ac.uk.

Part 2:
The Questions that
Need Answering

Chapter 9

Is Higher Education for All?

Is Higher Education for All?

'PEOPLE ARE BORN with talent and everywhere it is in chains. Fail to develop the talents of any one person, we fail Britain. Talent is twenty-first century wealth.' This quote is taken from Tony Blair's Labour Conference speech in Bournemouth in 1999. Within this policy rhetoric and the perspective of a 'knowledge-based economy', many are readily persuaded to move from brawn to brain. It is just a simple matter of removing the chains.

Professors Brown and Hesketh, in their recent book *The mismanagement of talent: employability and jobs in the knowledge economy* suggest that:

> The KBE [knowledge-based economy] conjures up a world of smart people, in smart jobs, doing smart things, in smart ways, for smart money, increasingly open to all rather than a few. Glossy corporate brochures present a future in challenging, exciting, and financially rewarding jobs for the winners in competition for fast track management appointments, offering training, self-development, and rapid career progression. They also convey an image of enlightened employers actively seeking to diversify their talent pool, reflected in their approach to identifying, hiring, and retaining outstanding people.[1]

However, thirty years ago Fred Hirsch, in a memorable line in his book *The social limits to growth*,[2] offered a different perspective: 'What each of us can achieve, all cannot.'

Millions of people are being asked to invest their time and money in a knowledge economy and the dream of equality of employment. In Chapter 1, the question of higher education for all – or for at least 50 per cent of school-leavers – was raised in relation to government policy and advancing the knowledge economy, and the Government's website (www.direct.gov.uk) is explicit as to the benefits of higher education: 'Attending university or college lets you experience a rich cultural and social scene and meet a variety of people, while studying something you love. Going into higher education can also lead to: a better paid job, a greater choice of job, higher future earning.' The emphasis is on the financial benefits and may sound to students like a good deal. It is easy for the young and enthusiastic to read 'can' as 'will'. But is the Government's primary concern for the welfare of students, or for the economy, or for employers? Or is it attempting to serve all three masters?

What are the practical and ethical limits guiding society, parents and universities in encouraging young people to enter higher education? If students go to university expecting major financial benefits in career progression, what happens if their expectations are not realised? And what happens to a university if it has contributed to unrealistic expectations? With the benefit of hindsight, perhaps we will have to acknowledge that a stronger case could have been made for our young people to enter instead the 'university of life'?

The unspoken question is: Will there be a life-chance without a university education? The answer is obviously yes, since most young people do not enter higher education. Statistics from the Higher Education Funding Council for England in 2005 indicate that over 60 per cent of young people in Scotland, London and the south-east of England do not enter higher education. In the rest of the country, the percentage rises to over 70 per cent. One can say with confidence that the absence of a formal university experience or qualification has not been a drawback to many people. Bill Gates is the world's richest man, creator of a huge commercial enterprise, and also the best-known university drop-out from the world's most highly ranked university, Harvard. He would presumably say that there are huge rewards in life outside a university education. Nearer to home, Sir Richard Branson, one of the UK's best-known businessmen and entrepreneurs, left school at 14 years of age. In November 2004 nearly 75 per cent of those taking part in a poll rated him the best financial role model in the UK.[3] The pages of history are full of those who never went to university, and indeed many who were not interested in, or failed at, formal education altogether: the Duke of Wellington, Sir Winston Churchill, Darwin, Einstein and countless others.

The annual listings of the most financially successful people in the UK attest that many have made their way to the top other than via a formal university education. Plumbers, engineers, hairdressers, restaurateurs, car mechanics, joiners, tailors and people from many other trades, vocations and professions, who opted for workplace apprenticeships ahead of university degrees, head the list of Britain's self-made millionaires: only two of the top 25 in the 2007 list went on to university after school.[4] Their success is inspiring and they have created valued opportunities for many others in our society. It is undisputed that for these people, lack of a degree has not proved an impediment. Mobile-phone billionaire businessman John Caudwell, who credits his apprenticeship for teaching him how to be a good businessman, recommends young people today to take a vocational qualification: 'If you want to be a professional, then you should get a degree, but if you want to be a businessman, go selling and start learning on the shop floor.'[5]

Whether such attainments reflect the potential of society in general is less certain. There is evidence that people with degrees do better financially than those without (see below). However, as touched on in Chapter 1, people choose to go to university for a number of different reasons, and potential students should aim to be clear about their expectations. It is easy to equate financial success with broader success and satisfaction in life. After all, making money and being miserable is a poor option. But what exactly makes a 'happier' future? In a consumerist society, the earning of more money is frequently and unthinkingly associated with greater happiness. But some find fulfilment in a life spent in self-sacrifice, helping the poor and needy. Is happiness found in prestige and power? Social status? Acquiring vast amounts of money and becoming a spendthrift – or a philanthropist? The list is endless.

Many student studies have been carried out on the equation between financial success and happiness, often termed 'quality of life' or 'life satisfaction'. Among US college students an orientation towards materialistic values is negatively associated with self-esteem, enjoyment of relationships, life satisfaction and affective experience.[6] These negative associations between materialism and well-being have been replicated in samples of Australian,[7] English,[8] German,[9] Russian,[10] Singaporean[11] and other students.[12] In his book *Happiness: lessons from a new science*, Richard Layard[13] presents an elegant, persuasive and up-to-date account of the recent evidence.

Alan Ryan, warden of New College, Oxford, in an article entitled 'What's wrong is that economists have become the hired helpers of governments bent on making us all work long hours for no good reason', records that more is never enough because we are betrayed by a subconscious setting in our brain: positional goods promise happiness that is unrealisable (i.e. 'if everyone wants to own the most expensive car on the block, all bar the (momentary) winner in the ostentation race lose out') and habituation means that any happiness attained does not last ('the first moments of gratification in our lives are intense and very pleasurable then the effect dies away'). In his words:

If what is produced does not in fact add to human happiness, having a lot more of it seems a bit pointless. What has this got to do with higher education? Indirectly, a lot... it suggests that our obsession with flexible labour markets may do more damage in producing stress and uncertainty than it does good in reducing unemployment so that turning higher education into a route into work by way of emphasising the need to keep on 're-tooling' may also be a mistake. It may even suggest that students sitting around doing nothing are sometimes doing exactly what they should be doing – working out what will make them happy over the next 60 years.[14]

Some graduates appear to have quietly worked it out exactly as Alan Ryan had hoped for. In a survey commissioned by Lloyds TSB, it was reported in January 2005 that graduates appear to be focusing on gap years, further study or working for themselves, rather than the corporate culture. In 2004, fewer than 4 per cent saw £1 million as something to aspire to, while four in ten regarded financial success as simply having 'enough to get by on'. Seventy-five per cent said financial know-how was the best guarantee of success, with luck (31%), education (27%) and family backing (16%) as other factors.[15] Paul Hyde of Lloyds TSB said: 'The get-rich-quick attitude many people might think exists in Britain seems to be largely a myth. Most people aspire to comfort rather than excessive wealth and hold high the value of hard work and a cautious approach to money.'[16]

Perhaps such graduates might share their thoughts with others for whom a successful outcome of education is still seen in terms of a solid and respected career with good financial returns, without too much thought or insight as to whether or not this represents future 'happiness' and 'satisfaction' in their lives.

But doesn't a degree confer financial advantage?

In daily discussions with students, a frequent reason that emerges for going to university is the belief that it will enhance job opportunities. This may or may not be related to a financial advantage. But the brief answer to this question, 'Does a degree confer financial advantage?', is a qualified yes, at least over the last half-century. The more education that people have received, the greater their income and the less likely they have been to experience unemployment. This has long been one good reason to go to university.

The Dearing Committee of Inquiry into UK Higher Education in 1997 estimated the rate of return as being between 11 and 14 per cent. The clear, consistent conclusion was that every year that a student remained in education beyond the school-leaving age increased income significantly.[17] This may also include or reflect the other benefits of enhanced intellectual, social and personal skills arising from a university education.

The benefits do not stop there. The more educated you are, the more likely you have been to enjoy stable, long-term employment. For example, in the UK men with less than a secondary education are at least three times more likely to be unemployed than those receiving a university education; the figures for women show them about twice as likely. Some care is required in interpreting these relative chances of being unemployed, bearing in mind prevailing unemployment rates, but nevertheless the trend is clear.

The increasing importance of qualifications was also underlined by the British Birth Cohort Studies carried out in 2000, which tracked the lives of 40,000 people born in one week in England, Scotland and Wales in 1946, 1955 and 1970. It was found that people without qualifications are more excluded from our society and live in greater poverty than 50 years ago, despite overall improvements in health, income and housing. Family income was almost twice as high for those with degrees in the 1970 cohort compared with those with no qualifications. In the 1946 cohort the gap was lower, at 30 per cent. Co-editor of the report, John Bynner commented: 'Life has become harder for those without qualifications. The old jobs for the unskilled... simply no longer exist'.[18]

As we progressed into the new millennium the news continued to be good. For example, the report in October 2003 by the Council for Industry and Higher Education (CIHE), representing the leaders of industry and academia, concluded that the demand for graduates was likely to exceed the growing numbers emerging with degrees. The report indicated that the average graduate earned about 17 per cent more than someone with two or more A levels, although specific earning differentials varied noticeably between types of employment (see Figure 9.1).[19]

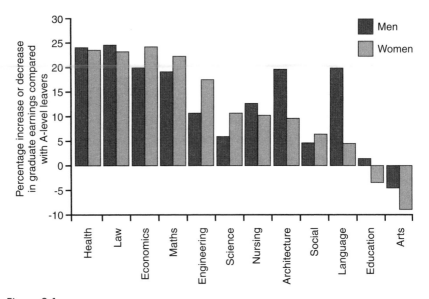

Figure 9.1

Source: Council for Industry and Higher Education (2003)

In the following year, a survey of more than 200 employers by the Association of Graduate Recruiters (AGR), representing an elite of 600 graduate employers, reported that the median graduate starting salary was expected to outstrip inflation. Carl Gilleard, AGR's chief executive claimed: 'Overall, it's an encouraging sign that employers are still prepared to pay a good market rate for graduate-level jobs. It does to some extent support the government's argument that you get a good return on your investment in higher education.' More than half of employers questioned, according to the report, said they were planning to increase the number of graduate vacancies that year.[20]

An OECD report in September 2004 also found a degree in the UK to be as valuable as ever. Graduates were earning 59 per cent more than non-graduates; they could expect to gain 10 per cent on their investment every year from graduation to the age of 65; and they were also more likely to find a job.[21] The OECD's 2006 report confirmed university graduates were in demand among employers in the UK and saw no evidence of demand being satisfied. The graduate premium, the salary differential for university graduates over secondary school leavers, was reported as 58 per cent, compared with 53 per cent in 1997.[22]

Few noticed that, in 2004, only 35 per cent of final-year students expected to enter the graduate job market, compared with 49 per cent in 1998. The number wanting to start their own business had risen from 35 to 43 per cent in five years. Also, major recruiters at the AGR conference on higher education in January 2004 were equally split on whether the UK was producing too many graduates. Slightly more than half believed that the expansion of higher education had adversely affected the quality of graduates.[23]

There were rumblings of distant thunder in the blue skies. For example in 2005, it was reported that companies were finding it difficult and expensive to attract top talent.[24] However, generally speaking, the good news continued. In September 2007, the *Sunday Times* announced:

> It's official: graduates are in demand by UK employers in 2007. Graduate vacancies are expected to increase by 12.7% this year, the fourth consecutive year that the number of job opportunities for graduates has gone up, according to the Association of Graduate Recruiters' (AGR) summer survey 2007. According to the Chartered Institute of Personnel and Development's 2007 recruitment, retention and turnover survey, 24% of 898 organisations responding had a structured graduate-recruitment programme. There's lots of competition among employers to sign up the most able and committed graduates in order to build a world-beating workforce of tomorrow.[25]

This and similar reports present a positive picture of the opportunities available for those completing higher education. Higher education appears to be an essential starting point on the road to fame and fortune. But for how many?

In *The mismanagement of talent* Professors Brown and Hesketh identified the reality of graduate salaries as follows: 'if the target of getting half of all young people through university is achieved, there are going to be huge numbers of graduates on low incomes unless there is a massive increase in the number of jobs paying higher wages'.[26] Then in July 2007 this prophecy appeared to be coming true. The AGR's annual summer survey reported:

> competition for jobs will be increasingly fierce, with an average of 29 applicants for each graduate vacancy in 2007. As a result employers are not increasing starting

salaries much above inflation because they are confident they will fill the positions. Although the salary increases predicted are fairly conservative, graduate salaries are already competitive in comparison to non-graduate entry level salaries.

The AGR's reported starting salary of £20,000 for graduates securing a job with one of the blue-chip organisations represented the average starting salary of only the top 5 per cent of the graduate labour market. Data from the Higher Education Statistics Agency show that 2005–06 first-degree graduates earned an average salary of around £18,000 in the UK – the same figure as for the previous year, despite increases in the cost of living. Salaries for graduates entering the market in 2007 are predicted to increase by a modest 2.4 per cent, to a median starting salary of £23,500.

It would appear that market forces not unreasonably control graduate salaries. The employers are rightly confident that graduates are in no position to argue about their salary level, because there appears to be an abundance of graduates, and employers can therefore dictate their terms. The year 2007 may subsequently be seen as a watershed in graduate employment, and future graduates may need to look to present and future trends rather than past experiences for a sanguine view of their prospects in the job market.

Chapter 10

What are a Student's Prospects?

What are a Student's Prospects?

A MAJOR EMPHASIS IN the Government's attempts to persuade young people to enter higher education has been on the improved prospects for employment that a degree is supposed to confer. This view is also promoted by employers. Universities, or at least their marketing departments, also encourage a belief in a link between higher education and future employment prospects. Academics themselves, however, are generally reticent on the subject: they see the incessant increase in student numbers affecting the employment market into which their graduates are moving.

Whilst it may have been true at times in the past that a university degree provided a passport to improved career opportunities and earnings, historic employment statistics may be seriously misleading when it comes to present and future prospects for the tens of thousands of students who now graduate every year. The Higher Education Statistics Agency (HESA) monitors graduate destinations. Their figures collected over a decade, and presented in Figure 10.1, show a drop in graduates who are in full-time work six months after graduating from just over two-thirds in the 1990s to slightly more than half in the first years of the twenty-first century.

The unemployment profiles may actually be worse than presented in the official statistics. For the HESA figures constitute students graduating in many disciplines, but those in, for example, healthcare have an almost 100 per cent employment rate. The percentage of students in other disciplines failing to get jobs must therefore be higher than 50 per cent. The availability of present-day employment opportunities and rewards is closely related to the subject studied at university. The 2007 report from the Association of Graduate Recruiters (AGR) indicated that the vacancies in accountancy and professional services (23%), followed by banking and financial services (12.2%), dominated the field.[1] Additionally, there is a geographical bias: over half (56.6%) of vacancies were in London and the South-East. HESA data for 2005–06 shows that of those in employment 26 per cent were in professional occupations, 30 per cent were in associate professional and technical jobs, 14 per cent were employed as administrators or secretaries and 10 per cent as sales or customer-service staff.

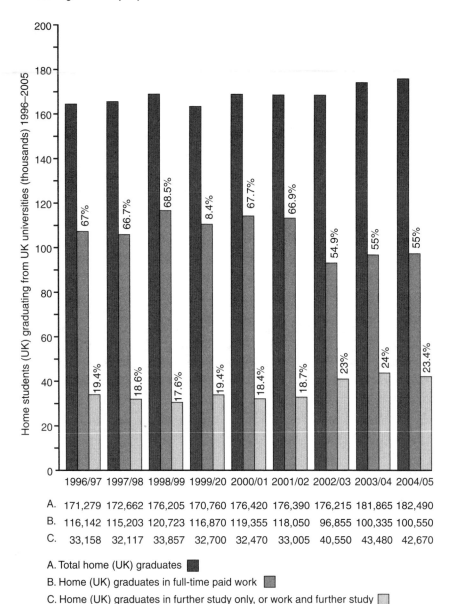

	1996/97	1997/98	1998/99	1999/20	2000/01	2001/02	2002/03	2003/04	2004/05
A.	171,279	172,662	176,205	170,760	176,420	176,390	176,215	181,865	182,490
B.	116,142	115,203	120,723	116,870	119,355	118,050	96,855	100,335	100,550
C.	33,158	32,117	33,857	32,700	32,470	33,005	40,550	43,480	42,670

A. Total home (UK) graduates ■

B. Home (UK) graduates in full-time paid work ■

C. Home (UK) graduates in further study only, or work and further study □

Figure 10.1 Graduating home (UK) students in full-time paid work or further study and work, 1996–2005

Source: HESA

This profile of UK graduate employment is, perhaps inevitably, similar to that recorded in America by Professor Berg nearly 40 years ago (see Chapter 1).

These figures raise further questions about what the 45 per cent or so of graduates who are not in full-time employment are doing. If we select the data for just a single year, 2002–03, further HESA figures show part of the answer – see Figures 10.2 and 10.3.

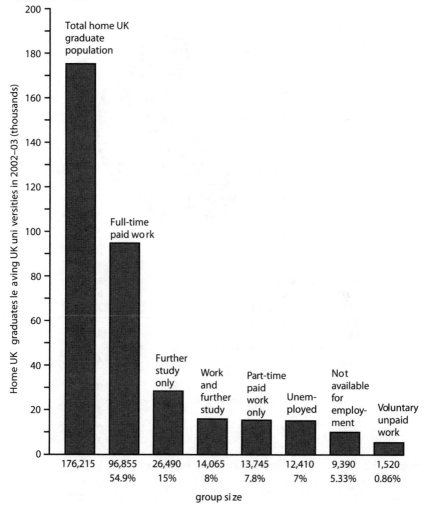

Figure 10.2 Destination of home (UK) undergraduates, 2002–03, six months after leaving university

Source: HESA

While not providing a complete picture, these figures do highlight the large number undertaking further study either full- or part-time, a trend continued in subsequent years' figures.

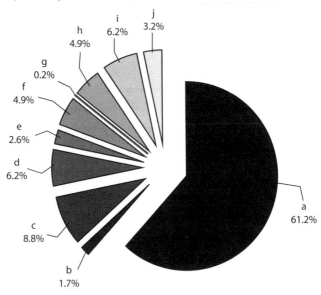

a:	In UK employment	61.2%
b:	In overseas employment	1.7%
c:	Working and studying	8.8%
d:	Studying in the UK for a higher degree	6.2%
e:	Studying in the UK for a teaching qualification	2.6%
f:	Undertaking other further study or training in the UK	4.9%
g:	Undertaking further study or training overseas	0.2%
h:	Not available for employment, study or training	4.9%
i:	Believed to be unemployed	6.2%
j:	Other	3.2%

Figure 10.3 'Destination of leavers from higher education' survey 2005
Source: HESA

Does this reflect an increasing motivation to develop further knowledge and skills, or a perceived need to enhance one's achievements above those of others seeking employment? Students at university may not know of the detailed HESA statistics, but most are fully aware of the serious limitations of a first degree when it comes to securing employment. The number of students progressing to further study may frequently represent an attempt to distinguish their CV from thousands of others.

But this is difficult to understand. What about all the exciting new jobs that the knowledge-based economy was supposed to generate?

Isn't the knowledge-based economy creating more jobs for graduates?

In the knowledge-based economy the USA has been the global leader, whom other nations aspire to emulate. But in an analysis of the US labour force between 1970 and 1995 Frederick Pryor and David Schaffer, in their book *Who's not working and why*, concluded that 'American workers have more education than is needed.'[2] The conclusions were in agreement with the official US Bureau of Labor Statistics, which published a report the following year accepting that no more than 30 per cent of all those working in America are in occupations that require a degree! The policy initiative of President Bush that was designed to develop the American workforce stated: 'Most new jobs will arise in occupations requiring only work-related training.'[3]

In *The mismanagement of talent*, Professors Brown and Hesketh provide a detailed analysis of the reality of the knowledge-based economy in the USA. They conclude:

> Our calculations suggest that the proportion of knowledge workers is set to increase only by two percentage points, or 3 million new jobs to 2010. This is not welcome news for the hundreds of thousands of college graduates hitting the US labor market each year, or for that matter, the 30 million workers in the United States who already hold a bachelor's or postgraduate degree qualification.[4]

In their analysis of the UK, they report that some 1.3 million people are likely to change jobs or retire each year. If approximately a third of these jobs are classed as 'knowledge-work occupations', it is estimated that each year

400,000 new graduates are competing for some 416,000 knowledge-worker posts with the 7.8 million graduates already at work in the UK: 'This might well account for why recent research suggests that as many as 40 per cent of graduates already are not actually using their university-acquired skills in their work.'[5]

In a review of the literature in 2005 on UK graduate employment, under-employment and unemployment, it was concluded that:

> The concept of over-education is difficult to define and measure precisely, but evidence from the 1980s, 1990s and today shows that even up to 10 years after graduating a significant number of graduates (around 30%) had never worked in jobs for which a degree is a formal requirement. In terms of graduate demand, therefore, the research evidence shows that a significant minority (approximately 30%) are under-employed. There was also evidence of significant and growing income differences between graduates in the labour market: 'those in poor quality jobs tended to be from non-traditional backgrounds – poorer homes or areas – and to have done less well at university'.[6]

It has been argued that the displacement of technicians and jobs for school leavers by jobs for graduates reflected employer requirements for higher levels of skills and knowledge. Graduates have better analytical and problem-solving skills than non-graduates.[7] However, as Professor Ivar Berg commented over 30 years ago in his book *Education and jobs: the great training robbery*:

> The most serious consequence of the educational upgrading of work opportunities is... the displacement of a significant population at the other end of the labour force, who must compete for jobs once held by people of modest educational achievement and with people whose educational achievements have gone up... There may be social/psychological benefits to people and organisations stemming from diplomas and degrees, but these benefits must be seen in a perspective that takes account of the consequences for the uncredentialed... In the meantime, we reward the highly educated with superior incomes on the grounds of their productive contribution.[8]

Of the 61 per cent of graduates identified as being in full-time employment in HESA's *Destination of leavers from higher education* survey in 2005 (see above), about 15 per cent moved into the 'traditional' graduate job categories of law, education and business/financial sectors. (The health sector – a traditional graduate destination for doctors and dentists – is an oddity, but the percentage also includes nurses, who are newer on the graduate scene.) The table below shows the distribution among all areas of employment.

Table 12.1 Destinations of leavers from higher education (breakdown of 61.2% in full-time employment)

Marketing, sales and advertising professionals	4.5%
Commercial, industrial and public-sector managers	9.5%
Scientific research, analysis and development professionals	1.1%
Engineering professionals	3.0%
Health professionals and associate professionals	13.2%
Education professionals	6.6%
Business and financial professionals and associate professionals	7.8%
Information technology professionals	4.0%
Arts, design, culture, media and sports professionals	5.8%
Legal professionals	0.7%
Social and welfare professionals	3.2%
Other professionals, associate professional and technical occupations	5.3%
Numerical clerks and cashiers	2.8%
Other clerical and secretarial occupations	11.7%
Retail, catering, waiting and bar staff	9.3%
Other occupations	11.5%
Unknown occupations	0.1%

Source: HESA

At least with hindsight, it was naive to believe that employers, in response to a greater number of educated graduates, would simply increase new jobs to develop quality goods or services. A large-scale survey revealed that during two decades (1981–99), the UK's workforce engaged in 'knowledge work' increased by only five percentage points.[9]

The 'knowledge-based economy': a false promise

Policy rhetoric and assumptions of employability in the 'knowledge-based economy' has become known to many, if not most students, as a false promise. Mass higher education has become the problem rather than the solution to future graduate employment. It is simple to understand by analogy. When relatively few people had a car, the drive to work was uneventful. If everyone has a car, road congestion ensures very slow progress – if you arrive at all. Some just give up.

Despite the reported growth in graduate jobs, the huge increase in graduate numbers has meant a reduction in opportunities for any one student. The AGR provides a figure of 29 applicants for every graduate vacancy, but this is an average of a wide range. For accountancy firms the figure is 10, for investment banks 26. The insurance sector reports, however, an average of 50 applicants for each graduate job on offer, while for consumer brand companies such as Unilever and Procter & Gamble the average figure is 104 graduates competing for each place. There are simply not enough graduate-level job opportunities. This means that graduates are in severe competition with other graduates and are competing for non-graduate jobs. Differences in income between graduates have become greater than those between non-graduates and graduates.[10]

Some may regard this as a healthy competition. But that is naive and misleading. For, however hard the graduates work, however many degrees they obtain, whatever the intensity of work experience or other business and social skills acquired, there simply will not be the opportunities to which they all aspire.

Many students have been persuaded to enter university on the expectation of better job opportunities or better salaries. It is surely more honest to indicate that the immediate employment prospects for many university graduates will be difficult, if not very difficult. Indeed, will many thousands of students have little chance, if any, of graduate-type employment? This understanding may engender a more realistic and determined student attitude, and avoid criticism of universities for misrepresentation.

In the meantime, students experience the reality of employment and unemployment without the conformist rhetoric. Here are just two views from the front lines:

> The AGR are wrong. They always offer warm glowing pictures of graduate pay and prospects by not being representative. The average median graduate starting salary by my reckoning is £12,000–13,000. I think the ratios are wrong too, far higher than 29:1. More like 75 or 100 to 1 like many jobs have been for years. The only thing they are right on is that employers are obsessed with psychometric tests.
>
> Paul, York, UK

> More testing? We're not human anymore, merely ciphers to fit some corporate bore's idea of what it is to be human. No doubt this testing is used by all of the most brain-dead corporate suits possible. And no wonder Apple can come out with the iPhone and leave these guys standing in the dust.
>
> John, Mountain View, California

With competition intense, all students are engaged in gaining positional advantage that has little relevance to their intellectual development and decreasing relevance to their educational credentials. It is not surprising that numerous reports and surveys in recent years have highlighted the number-one concern of university students to be not the debts, workloads or balancing academic, social and work commitments, but achieving the desired degree classification.

Chapter 11

What is the Employers' Perspective?

What is the Employers' Perspective?

THE AIM OF recruitment for any job is to select the best candidate, and selection is about fairly differentiating or discriminating (in the sense of discerning or being able to see fine distinctions) between different people, their past and present abilities, and purported future potential. This is an imperfect science.

The increasing number of graduates, and of universities, has exacerbated a genuine problem for even major companies in their search for the most promising employees. They simply do not have sufficient staff or time to visit every university. They are left with targeting certain universities from which, through habit or experience, they have previously obtained good employees. It remains for universities to convince employers that they have a 'quality product' and for employers to differentiate but not be prejudiced in the focus of their attentions.

For the 'elite' graduate employment opportunities, employers seek exceptional performance by exceptional candidates. At this level employers are competing with each other in what has been described as the 'war for talent',[1] and prestigious companies feel they need look no further than to our most prestigious universities, which has little to do with corporate rhetoric of 'equality of opportunity' or 'diversity'. In their book *The mismanagement of talent*, Professors Brown and Hesketh describe this as 'developing a few rather than nurturing the talents of all'. They record that:

> One leading employer in our research received over
> 14,000 applications for 400 places. Candidates applying
> from Oxford University were found to be 29 times more
> likely to get appointed than someone applying from a new
> (post-1992) university.[2]

This is despite the fact that, as Brown and Hesketh emphasise, the academic pecking order does not neatly map onto the hierarchy of managerial competence. This last observation opens up a whole new area of consideration and concern to which I will return, but let us stay for the moment with the fairness or otherwise of selectivity. In the wide-ranging doctorjob.com survey in 2003, students and graduates were asked: 'How do you feel about employers who target certain universities?' The respondants had mixed views, ranging from 'It makes perfect sense to me' to 'It makes me red with rage.' But, as Figure 11.1 shows, a breakdown of the comments between students from different universities revealed marked differences in response. Many more students from the 'new' universities felt aggrieved than from the 'old'.[3]

If employers deliberately choose to avoid applications from students from certain universities because past experience has proved such graduates are not appropriate, they are applying a rational basis for the bias and decision. However, this discrimination is likely to rest on statistical rather than individual distinctions. Employers therefore may well miss out on able individuals.

It is unlikely that employers would wish to offend the many stakeholders in higher education by overtly biasing their graduate selection towards particular universities. In any event online recruitment now provides an alternative which in theory affords a fairer way than visiting just certain universities. Recruiting any staff is an expensive business, and posting a vacancy on Prospects.

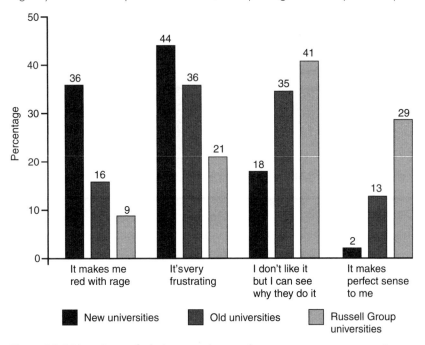

Figure 11.1 How do you feel about employers who target certain universities?
Source: doctorjob.com survey, March 2003

ac.uk or using Milkround.com can quickly run up substantial bills.[4] But it does give all graduates a chance to express an initial interest in opportunities for employment, irrespective of their geographical location. Online recruitment also gives all employers, small and large, a chance to compete. Going online is identified as an essential part of the modern graduate recruitment drive, with 76.9 per cent of 219 respondents to a survey by the Association of Graduate Recruiters accepting only online applications.[5] This is intended to make it easier for employers to readily distinguish the most academically able students, but mass higher education and degree inflation (see Chapter 7) has ensured that this has become fraught with difficulties as they are still faced with an avalanche of applications from graduates all with apparently similar grades of intellectual ability and talent. Graduating students are well aware that if they cannot tick the box showing at least a 2:1 degree, their application will probably be electronically rejected, but simple academic grading is no longer considered the most reliable sifting mechanism.

It has been known for some time that certain graduate employers have been using UCAS points (i.e. A-level results) rather than degree results to perform an initial screen of candidates. Not surprisingly, this has caused deep concern. Students coming from private education, with its superior levels of staffing and facilities, clearly achieve higher A-level grades, although these have not proved accurate predictors of final degree grades (see Chapter 3). The 2003 doctorjob.com survey also asked students how they felt about employers who use UCAS points to select candidates for jobs. Whilst there were differences in student responses (with notable variation between students at 'old', 'new' and 'Russell Group' universities), many students were clearly very angry or frustrated by this form of screening, which obviously negates the effect of the university experience. Around a third of students, however, said that although they did not like it they could see why employers do it. Furthermore, some said it made perfect sense. Whether this reflected a genuine concordance with the principle of using A-level grades for initial selection or simple self-interest by those with presumably better A-level grades, only the students themselves could clarify.[6]

But does it make 'perfect sense'? For it to do so, the employers would have to show that there was a correlation between A-level grades and the relative success of the chosen candidates in employment. Employers may have this information, if indeed it exists, but it would not appear to be published. What *does* exist is a study in 1975 of an investigation of Harvard graduates in the fields of law, medicine, teaching and business, which found that scores on entrance exams had zero or negative correlation with their eventual career success.[7] Possibly a Harvard intake of students is atypical of a broader church of student entry, but it would appear imperative that employers establish with transparent clarity, for both students and themselves, the validity of using UCAS points to judge future success.

To suggest that a person's A-level grades accurately define even academic potential creates individual anomalies (see Chapter 7). But to suggest that A-level grades are the defining feature of individual potential in the market place or in life is simply wrong. When attempts are made to correlate IQ test scores with performance in careers, the highest estimate of the difference attributed to IQ is about 25 per cent.[8] Other studies suggest lower values of 4 to 10 per cent.[9] At best this leaves 75 per cent of success in working life attributable to other factors.

This is borne out in a long-term study that began 50 years ago. In the 1950s, eighty PhD students in science received an intensive series of psychological and IQ tests and interviews to assess emotional balance, integrity, interpersonal effectiveness and other attributes. Some forty years later in 1994, detailed estimates were made of each person's career success and the reasons for the success established. Emotional intelligence abilities were identified as being some four times more important than IQ in determining professional success and prestige.[10]

With an average 29 applicants for every position (and, as we have seen, a great many more in some areas of employment), employers need rapidly to be able to eliminate 28. It has been accepted for many years that 'first-class brains do not necessarily make first-class managers'. Alongside 'hard skills' measured in IQ terms, such as numeracy, numerical reasoning and logic, employers require the 'softer' skills of communication, confidence, planning and organisation, passion and other attributes.[11] These necessarily become the tools of elimination. To reduce applicants to a manageable number, online psychometric tests are brought in at the application stage – this type of testing has normally been reserved for interview.

The summer graduate recruitment survey carried out by the Association of Graduate Recruiters (AGR) in 2007 found that 91 per cent of employers place 'considerable confidence' in psychometric testing in the recruitment process. John Rust, director of Cambridge University's Psychometrics Centre, said: 'Increasingly employers have to [use psychometric tests] because degree classification is such a variable quantity these days and they are so broad and in

very different subjects. Employers can't tell [a graduate's] competencies fro...
their degree.'[12]

Dr Daniel Goleman, who has written so interestingly and persuasively on 'emotional intelligence' (EQ), was against the unthinking use of his model, with its list of competencies, in application forms, interview questions and so forth: 'I think people have to be very careful. I think that the really good executive recruiters, for instance, are people who have emotional intelligence and who recognise it in others. But I don't think you should use the model for any kind of selection test.' When questioned on the EQ test he added: 'There are several self-report tools that are being sold as tests of emotional intelligence, but I think it would be a big mistake to use any of them for selection, if only because the first domain of emotional intelligence is self-awareness. If someone is low on that ability, how are you going to trust any of their other self assessments.'[13]

Dr Goleman's concerns are substantiated in a study by Janovics and Christiansen in 2001 that indicated that self-report measures of EQ were of little practical value in predicting performance at work in a sample of 176 employed undergraduate students.[14] In a classic publication in 1973, entitled 'Testing for competence rather than intelligence', D.C. McClelland argued that traditional academic aptitude, school grades and further qualifications simply did not predict people's job performance or success in life.[15] It was proposed that a number of specific 'competencies' or traits including self-discipline, empathy and initiative distinguished the most successful people from those who simply maintained a job. It triggered a huge and continuing research interest in how to better measure and encourage human potential in the workplace and in life.

In a national survey of what employers are looking at for entry-level workers, specific skills are listed as less important than the ability to learn on the job. This ability included: listening and oral communication, adaptability and creative responses to set backs and obstacles, personal management, confidence and motivation to work towards goals, a sense of wanting to develop one's career and take pride in accomplishments, cooperativeness and team work, and wanting to make a contribution.[16] These are similar to the three most desired capabilities that corporations are seeking in the MBAs they hire: communication skills, interpersonal skills and initiative.[17] Social skills may become the determining factor in employment success. Prospective candidates may have to show qualities that, to quote Brown and Hesketh, 'in a previous life may have resulted in canonisation'.

The AGR's survey states: 'For many AGR employers, the days of academic criteria as the be-all and end-all are long gone; despite this fact, the extent to which some of them appear to be reducing emphasis on this side of things is interesting — particularly against the background of the "grade inflation" phenomenon.'

Some organisations are looking to 'focus more on soft skills and to put more faith in the selection process — and hence, one might infer, less faith in the ability of degree classes to accurately mirror the graduate competences that matter.'[18]

These comments relate to skills and attributes that might perhaps be considered the remit of universities to teach, but there is also evidence of a loss of faith in the academic abilities expected to be part and parcel of higher education. In her book *Does education matter?* Professor Alison Wolf is clear: 'One result of the recent university explosion is that many of those entering graduate jobs probably do so with lower skill levels than in previous years, since their studies are less well funded and less effective.'[19] One company in the AGR's 2007 survey said it was planning to introduce verbal and numerical reasoning tests — which fall firmly at the 'hard academic' end of the skills continuum — because 'degree qualifications are not a reliable indicator of this aptitude'.[20]

Phillip Brown, professor of social sciences at Cardiff University and co-author of the previously quoted *The mismanagement of talent*, summed up a widely observed tendency in an article in the *Times Higher Education Supplement*. He noted that, whereas education has traditionally rationed access to high-skilled and high-waged employment by the credential of a university degree, this is being revealed as of depreciating interest. It is the social and other competencies and skills that are in the ascent.[21]

In truth, the latter may have long played the determinant role in many prestigious appointments, but presumably this was not what was intended by those who envisaged educational ennoblement through a mass higher-education system.

Universities may view such developments with dismay and fear. If the views expressed by the AGR and expert commentators come to reflect the views of all employers in the UK, universities become, at best, secondary players in the employment stakes. How long will it be before the reducing emphasis on degrees essentially renders academic credentials unsafe? It will then perhaps be time to review the role of a university education.

Chapter 12

Why Do So Many Students Make Wrong Choices?

Why Do So Many Students Make Wrong Choices?

What difference does it make what university you choose?

Brown and Hesketh's observation that 'the academic pecking order does not neatly map onto the hierarchy of managerial competence' (see Chapter 11) means that employers cannot simply assume that a graduate from a 'top university' is right for them. Similarly, prospective students should not take it for granted that getting into a 'top university' will be a meal ticket to success.

Professors Sally Power, Geoff Whitty and Tony Edwards have been following 300 educationally promising young people since the start of their secondary schooling in the 1980s, when they were considered destined for success. They are now in their early 30s. The team found that most had fulfilled their promise but that educational background made a difference to the degree of success.

Four in ten (41%) of those who had gone to elite universities were in the top social class, compared to just under three in ten (28%) of those who had gone to non-elite old universities and fewer than one in ten (8%) of those from new universities. Only five per cent of those from old universities had not secured professional or managerial occupations, compared to over a fifth (22%) of the new university graduates. There was also a relationship between the status of the university attended and the type of further study: fewer than one in ten from a new university had progressed to a master's degree and none had done a PhD. But over one-fifth from old universities had master's degrees and one in ten had a PhD.

According to the study, 'Meritocratic arguments could be used to explain the connection between schooling and earnings, as privately schooled respondents obtained higher A-levels and more went to Oxbridge.'[1] 'However, as a journalist commented, 'the legacy of private education is also evident in the relative success of a small group who did not go to university, which suggests that an elite private education confers advantages other than high levels of academic attainment'.[2] Professor Power observed that, 'The research shows the enduring legacy of an elite education. Going to a prestigious private school and university appears to bring strong occupational and financial advantages.' Professor Whitty added: "The huge challenge facing the government's widening participation agenda is evident from the research.'[3]

If the authors' conclusions are correct, then private education can rejoice in the warm glow of satisfaction (and relief) of a job well done. The expense of a private education is vindicated. Similarly, the 'elite' universities who have not hidden their wishes to charge undergraduates far more for the 'privilege' of a 'superior education' can also breathe a sigh of relief. Or can they?

The fundamental challenge is to distinguish the inherent ability of the student from the added value of the school or university. Do students bring to universities more than universities bring to students? In a provocative article entitled 'The worthless Ivy League?' *Newsweek's* business columnist Robert Samuelson identified the problem:

> We all 'know' that going to college is essential for economic success. The more prestigious the college, the greater the success. It's better to attend Yale or Stanford than, say, Arizona State. People with the same raw abilities do better and earn more by graduating from an elite school. The bonus flows (it's said) from better connections, brighter 'peers,' tougher courses or superior professors. Among many parents, the terror that their children won't go to the 'right' college has supported an explosion of guidebooks, counselors and tutoring companies to help students in the admissions race.
>
> The trouble is that what everyone knows isn't true. Going to Harvard or Duke won't automatically produce a better job and higher pay. Graduates of these schools generally do well. But they do well because they're talented. Had they chosen colleges with lesser nameplates, they would (on average) have done just as well. The conclusion is that the Ivy League – a metaphor for all elite schools – has little comparative advantage. They may expose students to brilliant scholars and stimulating peers. But the schools

don't make the students' success. Students create their own success; this makes the schools look good.[4]

Samuelson based his argument on evidence from a study carried out by Alan Krueger, an economist at Princeton, and Stacy Berg Dale, a researcher at the Andrew W. Mellon Foundation. In questioning the generally held opinion that an elite education equated with higher earning power and greater success, Krueger and Dale followed the destinies of students entering 34 colleges of varying status across America in 1976. Previous studies had found that going to an elite college did give graduates a modest boost beyond what their pre-university abilities suggested, but Krueger and Dale suspected that this might be a 'statistical quirk', and that 'students who attend more elite colleges may have greater earnings capacity regardless of where they attend school'.[5] They believed studies to date had not taken into account inherent qualities, such as ambition and perseverance that admissions staff were discerning in their choices of student. Factoring in these elements, Krueger and Dale found no difference in the average earnings of former students of the same ability, irrespective of where they went to university. (The only exception was poorer students, who did move slightly up the scale if they went to an elite university.) Samuelson concluded:

> Once you're in the job market, where you went to college may matter for a few years, early in your career. Companies don't know much about young employment candidates. A shiny credential (an Ivy League degree) may impress. But after that, what people can or can't do counts for more. Skills grow. Reputations emerge. Companies prefer the competent from Podunk to the incompetent from Princeton.

It is particularly interesting to hear that no less than 40 per cent of students did not simply accept the first and most prestigious university offer that came along.[6] They chose another university and did just as well. And these were able students. If sufficient students followed this example, employers would finally have to follow the students. The present procedures that positively or negatively discriminate between students or between their universities would then decrease.

This is not to say, however, that students should be careless in their choice of university. Rather, they should choose the right one *for them*. This will largely reflect four different but inter-related strengths:

- personal interest, motivation and application – what we enjoy most we usually do best;
- the skill of the teachers and their ethos in teaching and learning;
- the relevance and quality of the course;
- the 'standard' of the degrees at a particular institution.

It seems a simple formula, but in fact it is fraught with difficulties, and many of the disappointments and frustrations that students experience, especially in their first year, is linked to making wrong choices, often through no fault of their own.

Reasons why students make poor choices

Evidence that tens of thousands of students make ill-informed decisions about their higher education is borne out by the number who drop out from their university course: on average no less than one in ten students. In the first annual Student Survey, conducted by the doctorjob.com in March 2003, when asked, 'Would you have chosen to go to a different university, knowing what you know now?' one in four graduates replied: Yes. Six out of ten graduates said that, if they could have had their time over again, they would have considered doing a different degree.

With over two hundred UK universities and colleges awarding degrees, and many thousands of courses on offer, the difficulties in the selection of a subject, course and university are self-evident. Wrong choices are an important factor in 'dropping out', and league tables using retention rates make for uncomfortable reading. Some universities face a drop-out rate as high as 30 per cent.

But with all the information that is now available, and with all the advice given from family, friends, school, universities and elsewhere, how is it possible for so many inappropriate decisions to have occurred? The report by Curtis and Attwood[7] identified the top four factors which most influenced students' thinking in their choice of university:

- course content
- entry grades required
- location of the university
- reputation of the university.

Clearly, then, there is some discernment in student choice. Yet there must be concern that students are relying heavily on marketing material that is specifically designed to be persuasive of a specific university, with little in the way of comparative information between universities and courses.

For most current students it is probable that the choice of university will have related heavily, directly or indirectly, to two factors:

- the perceived character and academic reputation of the university and its social strengths;

- the perceived quality and nature of the undergraduate course in preparing students for a future career.

These two perceptions are frequently influenced by peer, family or school pressure.

It is reasonable that both these factors will be perceived as especially important. However, difficulties remain in interpreting information from a prospectus and other material, or even from a visit to a university, or from the well-meaning guidance of career advisors or friends. All such advice remains relevant, but for most students it is unlikely that family or friends, who may have completed their education some time ago, have up-to-date and inside knowledge to compare institutions and subjects or courses sensibly. Meanwhile, information available from individual universities should be approached with considerable care; from them you will only receive the good news.

In a survey in 2005, undertaken by the research company Opinionpanel, the perceptions and preferences of 10,000 first-year students regarding their choice of university provided a student's view of how universities performed during the application process. The survey also registered whether institutions had been recommended by teachers and parents. The students were canvassed for views about universities' academic reputation, teaching quality, campus facilities and location. They were also asked to indicate, on a scale of one to seven, their perception of staff helpfulness. The results suggest that location can be a decisive factor in students' choice of where to study. Some 80 per cent of under 21-year-olds said that 'a friendly campus feel' was important to their choice, while 72 per cent said going to a university with the image of being 'strong in league tables' was important. Old universities dominated the top ten student-rated institutions in most categories – with Oxford, Cambridge and London colleges perceived as having the best academic reputations. In the ten key topics covered by the survey, Strathclyde University received the greatest number of high-ranking positions – appearing in the top ten for students' perception of course quality, employment prospects and being an 'affordable' place to study. The University of Wales, Bangor, received the highest ratings for 'helpful administration' while Warwick University was seen as having the best campus. Several post-1992 universities were also highly rated by students in terms of marketing style and how they dealt with applicants. Ben Marks, managing director of Opinionpanel, said the study was intended to help admissions and marketing staff understand why students accept or reject offers. 'The sample size is large enough to yield robust findings at an institutional level. It's not really a tool for students. But it can help universities get their marketing right.'[8]

But it is not at all clear how freshers can distinguish in an informed way between 'academic reputation', 'league table' data and undergraduate needs. Indeed, Hannah Essex, the National Union of Students' vice-president (education), said: 'Students have different expectations and needs. While league tables make for interesting reading, prospective students need to look behind the rankings and assess whether the institution truly caters for their needs.'[9] In Chapter 4 we have looked at the ways in which league tables do and don't help.

How do school leavers assess whether an institution 'truly caters' for their needs? In interviews with more than 100 early leavers at universities in the north of England poor course selection was found to be the key factor in the decision to quit, particularly at post-1992 universities.[10] Research undertaken for the Learning and Skills Council similarly identified that recruiting underqualified candidates to inappropriate courses was the main reason students dropped out of university and college. The students surveyed complained that they had received inadequate advice on careers, university lifestyle and study skills because selectors had not been honest enough. It was considered that pressures on admission tutors and staff to recruit students in a 'bums-on-seats' policy may have contributed to the difficulties.[11] This reflects misrepresentation and an obvious lack of integrity which demeans higher education. It is obviously not acceptable, but reveals the pressure that may be placed on staff to do the wrong thing.

An 'impartial academic' would probably suggest that whilst an important consideration for students in their choice of subject and university is the reputation of the institution, it is important to distinguish between 'research reputation' and the 'teaching/learning reputation'. As we have seen in Chapter 5 they are not the same. Furthermore, it is the course syllabus and the quality and style of teaching which should be a pivotal focus of attention. In brief, in an ideal world students need to know who will teach them best and who has the best learning environment so that they will learn most! In the plethora of facts and figures these are factors which students may miss out on in their information-gathering. But this is hardly the fault of the student and his or her advisors: detailed information on course structure and teaching styles or quality are usually difficult for potential applicants to obtain; they may also be hard to assess.

Professor Derek Bok, a former president of Harvard University, offers a view as relevant to students entering UK higher education as it was to the American students he was addressing:

> If students could easily find out which colleges and
> professional schools would teach them the most (and if they
> were sensible enough to make these findings a decisive
> factor in their choice of schools to attend), the outcome [to
> improve teaching standards] might be different. The actual
> situation on university campuses today, of course, is a far
> cry from the one just described. No reliable method yet
> exists that allows students to determine where they will learn
> the most. Since applicants are generally hard-put to know
> just how much they are really learning, let alone how much
> they can expect to learn at a school they have never seen,
> they do not make enlightened choices. They rarely possess
> either the time or the information to explore all the promising
> options available to them and usually have only a limited
> basis for comparing the options they do consider... Indeed,
> students often flock to courses with superficial appeal or
> to institutions with established reputations even though the
> education they receive is only mediocre.[12]

A further concern is that choice of a university is influenced or compromised by earlier decisions, such as choice of A levels. A poll by ExamAid and the Association of Colleges (AoC) of 2,700 students aged 15 to 19 years, who were mostly in further education colleges, revealed that many believed that they had made the wrong choice of GCSEs or A levels. Nine per cent of students said they would like to change all or most of their subjects, 46 per cent said they wanted to abandon some of their chosen courses and more than a quarter taking AS and A levels were unsure whether they would complete at least one of their subjects. Judith Norrington, the AoCs director of curriculum and quality, said that students needed access to better advice when choosing their AS and A level subjects.[13]

The survey also showed that 80 per cent of students had taken the decision on their own,[14] a point picked up by Susan McGrath, education liaison officer at Manchester Metropolitan University, in a survey she did of 500 sixth-formers in Manchester. She found that 45 per cent of young people rely on school friends still at school or college for advice rather than teachers or parents, when choosing which university to attend. The advice of careers tutors and parents was sought by only about one third of the students, notwithstanding that the right advice was available in all four of the institutions from which the survey sample came.[15]

Finally, an influence identified in Chapter 3 should not be overlooked: that of advising pupils to take subjects such as psychology, rather than sciences or languages, because it is considered more difficult to achieve high A level grades in the latter. (The number of graduates in psychology increased 110 per cent between 1995 and 2005, while chemistry dropped 29 per cent, which seems to reflect this trend.)[16] The important issue of choices within secondary education is beyond the scope of this book, but parents and pupils, schools, universities and their academic staff and employers need to address the problem as a matter of urgency to help students better identify a more appropriate choice of A levels. Susan McGrath and colleagues suggest that advice about university study begin earlier and that targeted liaison between schools and universities would benefit students significantly.[17] Related to these issues, some universities are already targeting primary-school children in inner-city areas who have a low rate of participation in higher education.[18]

Making the right choice of course and university is essential. Academic staff, with their unique knowledge and subject expertise, should redouble their efforts to inform schools, teachers and parents of the reality of university life in order to help students make a more informed choice. A carefully considered choice of university and subject should greatly reduce the possibility of mistakes and much regret.

Chapter 13

Is Parent Power a Reality?

Is Parent Power a Reality?

PARENTS HAVE THE potential to influence, directly and indirectly, the success or demise of higher education. Their direct influence is attained by, first, helping to identify with their son or daughter a suitable course and university, and then providing the encouragement to apply. This is an invaluable role: they know their offspring better than anyone else. The indirect influence of parents is a stakeholder role in paying taxes. Presumably, they require value for money from the educational system. As voters they can also influence political opinion. If used wisely, this influence could be a potent force to assist higher education in the provision of teaching and learning.

The parental influence is indeed foundational to educational achievement as it relates to their ability to balance the varied skills required to ensure the single most important and consistent characteristic of happy children: that they have secure and loving relationships with their parent(s) and have empathy, with reasonable social and emotional competencies with other children:[1]

- Such crucial skills are a stronger predictor of children's future success than narrow measures such as exam grades.

- Having loving and supportive parents makes a bigger difference to children's educational attainment than which school they attend.

- Good family relations in childhood have a bigger influence on an individual later career success than how well they did in school.

- On average, in terms of parenting styles, children of authoritative parents are happier, more successful and better adjusted than children of authoritarian, indulgent or uninvolved parents.[2]

Many parents may be both pleased and yet disturbed to read that their own influence can so potently influence their children's success in life – even more than the school attended. But whilst parents have been welcomed into nursery, primary and secondary education, even if only for the fees they have paid, traditionally they have been ignored by higher education. Indeed, their presence has not been welcomed. A parent may have been invited to attend with their son or daughter on their interview or open day for a place at college or university. But the second and final brief parental appearance at college or university was almost certainly for their son's or daughter's graduation day! And how many academic staff did the parent meet on this occasion, to discuss the course and any questions or suggestions that they might have had to improve the educational provision? This is notwithstanding that many parents are highly successful professionals or come with a tremendous breadth of knowledge and life skills.

Universities have appeared indifferent, nervous or apprehensive about involving parents too closely. If this seems an unnecessarily harsh verdict, consider the views expressed by a departmental administrator at the University of York in an amusing article offering advice on how to deal with parents:

> Not content to deliver them for interviews and open days
> parents... take part in the process. Paying customers with
> an urgent need to sample the product. You can almost hear
> them slapping open their wallets and counting the cost of
> educating their little darlings, as they attend introductory
> lectures and tut-tut their way around campus... if there is any
> suggestion that, as teachers or bureaucrats, we have fallen
> short of our responsibilities by failing to interact dynamically
> with our charges... the fiery flames of litigation may await
> us. When the phone rings, and the caller announces
> themselves as mother or father of Tarquin or Christabel,
> there is an audible intake of breath. Is this the moment of
> reckoning?... What you have to do is practise an air of
> defiant nonchalance, cross your fingers and hope that the
> only time you meet the parents is to celebrate graduation
> day.[3]

If you remain uncertain as to the reception of parents by higher education, an editorial in the same publication the following year, entitled 'Parents must keep out', dispelled any doubts. It considered that:

> universities do students no favours by pandering to parents
> when their offspring are adults, with a right to privacy and
> plenty of procedures available to make a case for themselves
> when necessary. Becoming an independent thinker is a vital
> part of the higher education experience.[4]

Do parents really believe that they will be divorced from having to help their sons and daughters financially whilst at university? Do parents really believe that their sons and daughters facing a powerful institutional conglomerate really have 'plenty of procedures available to make a case for themselves', especially when some universities are attempting to reduce students' legal rights (see Chapter 8)? Do parents (or academic staff) really believe that a teenager has their intellectual and social experience to engage in equal combat and have the same influence as themselves? Or, to put it another way, do academic staff have the intellectual ability and social experience of an eighteen-year-old? Such views as those quoted seem disingenuous.

Parental experience across the Atlantic is very different. There, parents have firmly established their role in higher education, and an established advocacy group, College Parents of America, easily accessed from the Internet, deals with the college search, campus life and issues, and a myriad of other matters relevant to a student entering college or university. Universities have had to face and adapt to a highly vocal, and at times overbearing, parental presence.

In an article entitled 'Big mother is watching you', parents in America were described as becoming 'so demanding about everything from the colour of their child's room to exam grades that administrators have been forced to respond with special liaison officers and programmes to keep mum and dad in the loop about their child's life on campus'. Scott Chesney, assistant vice-president for student and academic services at the University of New Hampshire, was reported as saying that students' parents involved themselves on their child's behalf in everything from room-mate squabbles upwards: 'The big question is, do we deal with this reality and embrace parents as partners, or do we try to fight it and help students become more independent?' 'We've come to realise this is the way it's going to be,' said Gwendolyn Dungy, executive president of the National Association of Student Personnel Administrators. 'Universities are recognising that parents will be involved, whether they're welcomed or not.' Karen Levin Coburn, assistant vice-chancellor for students at Washington University, St Louis, who recalled a student arriving on campus with mother and interior designer in tow to decorate her room, says: 'They might as well make them understand how university works, so it can be a constructive relationship rather than an adversarial one.'[5]

This, perhaps, sounds a note of caution as well as inspiration, but if parents could collate their activities, as has occurred in America, the focus could influence an institution or course to flourish or close. I am *not* arguing to reduce the growing independence of a younger mind. Nor am I attempting to provide a licence for a parent to interfere improperly with the university–student relationship. Both students and universities would rightly resent such interference. Not merely would students resent the inappropriate appearance of their parents, most would die of embarrassment! But universities, parents and students can all benefit from greater mutual understanding and cross-fertilisation.

Some 15 years ago, when I was head of a department, a random selection of the students' parents were invited to a departmental open day, to show them the operation of day-to-day life in the university. As expected, some parents had not themselves been to university; of those that had, their experience was often 20 or 30 years out-of-date. The open day for parents was repeated on a subsequent occasion. The objective was to better inform them of the actuality of the teaching, learning and research environment of a modern university. Parents found the modern educational environment of interest and many were clearly surprised by the breadth of activities and responsibilities expected of the students and academic staff. No parent attempted to subvert the occasion for a familial concern. It was considered that such information might be valuable to them in their discussions on education in the real world; in short, it provided the potential for making major stakeholders in higher education into useful luminaries, partners or ambassadors.

Universities are beginning tentatively to acknowledge the parental role. Sheffield is one that refashioned its traditional open-day format several years ago. Paul Govey, Sheffield's head of UK and European Union recruitment, explained:

> To be honest, the parents are key stakeholders. So them
> bringing their kids to the university is the way we see things
> going now… we wanted a more face-to-face friendly
> approach and to avoid giving the impression that we are the
> bastions of academia with our gates shut to outsiders. We
> do not want to seem mysterious, or like we are saying, 'Give
> us your child and you will see them in three years.'[6]

Parents' views are of increasing importance with respect to escalating student fees, a steep rise in the number of students living at home, apprehension about potential bias and prejudice by universities in the selection of applicants, apprehension about potential bias by employers in the selection of applicants from certain universities, and general concerns about the value for money in higher education. The protest group Parents Against Cuts at Exeter (PACE) ensured that the students' predicament hit the headlines when Exeter University announced it was to discontinue chemistry and music courses. PACE involved the support of academic staff, students, school teachers and others, and showed how strongly parents can react when they have been seriously offended by the behaviour of a university and are determined to right a wrong for all students, not only their own kin.

If parents are armed by academic staff with an authoritative understanding of the real world of higher education, then parents' rights might be developed into responsibilities. This would have three major advantages.

- Together with their son or daughter parents can facilitate a more informed and balanced choice of university, college and course, to reduce the present numerous errors of judgement.

- Parents can help to better prepare a son or daughter for the realities of university life. It is curious that student university guides may have been of some merit in choosing a course and university. But having helped to place a student in university, the success or failure of the following years is frequently left to the student.

- While maintaining an unobtrusive or inconspicuous position with respect to their paternal concerns, parents as stakeholders, taxpayers and voters may wish to bring their influence to bear to encourage, maintain and improve standards in the provision of teaching and learning.

In summary, there is a reasonable concern by UK universities that parents should not interfere with the normal interaction of students with university, and still more that the parent–university engagement should not degenerate to an adversarial relationship. Yet a parent who complained about the number of tutor contact-hours that her daughter was receiving; or the mother who wrote that her daughter, at a world-renowned university, 'only gets three hours of teaching periods'; or the Scottish academic who said that 'parents and students have no concept of the demands placed on today's academics [when] teaching is sidelined', may give rise to serious concern worthy of an explanation. Surely it is worthwhile informing students and parents as to the realities of university life.

That parents will in the future increasingly play a more prominent role in the student's university experience is almost inevitable. There are two reasons linked to a common cause. As financial pressures have increased, many parents will be directly involved even more with the financial support of their sons and daughters at university. They will inevitably become a major stakeholder in higher education. But there is a corollary. In the attempt by government to reduce the cost of higher education, no less than 25 per cent of students now live at home. Whether they like it or not, many parents will not merely have a ring-side seat to observe the consequences of their son's or daughter's daily exposure to higher education: they may become daily participants.[7]

Chapter 14

What Can Make a Difference?

What Can Make a Difference?

STUDIES USING A variety of different critieria, both objective and subjective, have found that the most important positive correlations of student satisfaction with college and university life, learning and completing a degree, are:

- a faculty with a clear student orientation and commitment to teaching;
- the support of the student's peer group.

There is, however, a third important factor:

- the socio-economic status of the parent/student, which influences much of the academic and social experience.

The first two factors can be sought out and encouraged within the choice of university, course and department (see below). The third factor is problematic. Socio-economic circumstances, in whatever context, are issues of immense sensitivity and complexity that have implications far beyond the walls of higher education. However, having to undertake remunerated work whilst studying, and having to commute daily to university rather than living on campus or in a student house, have both been shown to have an adverse effect on student satisfaction and academic success.[1] While one or both of these factors may not always be avoidable, awareness of their negative effect may allow admissions tutors to be more realistic in the advice offered and help given to students and their parents.

As has been underlined earlier, negative influences, dissatisfaction and poor choices can increase drop-out rates and affect academic performance, resulting in degree ratings that may give an unfair or inaccurate indication of actual ability.

What can academic staff do?

This book has emphasised how important it is to make sure that students who wish to go to university make the right choice of subject, course, learning style and university. Academic staff, with their unique knowledge and subject expertise, could play an invaluable role in this process. Some already do, visiting schools, dealing with admission queries and contributing to department and university open days. This role is invaluable in providing the all-important demonstration to teachers, schools, students and parents that the academic staff, as well as the university, regard the admission procedures as of pivotal importance. It also shows that the department and university takes very seriously their responsibility to help prospective students and their parents in the choice of study in higher education and the quality of the undergraduate experience.

Academic staff need to present up-to-date and honest information which helps students to make a more informed choice. This will reap rewards as well-informed students will be better prepared for the daily reality of university life. If they feel confident that they have made the right choice, they will learn, progress and blossom. Regret, on the other hand, is quickly followed by dissatisfaction, which rebounds on the staff, who are faced with unhappy students. Unhappy students, like anyone else, expect things to go wrong, look for others to blame and are distracted by anything that can take their mind away from the cause of their unhappiness. Together with the support staff in the university, the inevitable time involved in counselling those who realise that they should not be there is considerable.

Prospective students may best be considered as 'clients' (see Chapter 8), and a professional always acts in the best interests of his or her clients. With the assumption that teachers in higher education are 'professionals', it is simply a question of integrity and doing the right thing. Also and at least as important, an honest staff–student interaction will empower academic staff and students (and parents) to maintain or restore the quality of undergraduate education, and so contribute to the improvement of teaching standards and the university experience. These are ambitious goals.

What can students do?

Students alight on a choice of university for many reasons: it may appear prestigious and promise a halo effect of reflected glory; they may, for financial or other reasons, wish to remain at home and choose a local university; or they may simply go along with peer group, school or family pressures. It happens – all the time. All such choices reflect a compromise as in life itself.

School-leavers require reliable information that should enable them to assess four distinctive but interrelated aspects of higher education.

- Will the student enjoy working and perhaps living within a particular university? Will it facilitate his or her teaching and learning, because successful learning is greatly influenced by our motivation and whether we feel comfortable and happy with our surroundings? Will it help the student to develop and broaden his or her intellectual, social and personal skills and cultural interests – and above all, to have fun!

- Will the teaching that a student receives be of high quality and be delivered by professional staff with a serious commitment to teaching and student learning – or is it delegated to others?

- Will the course or curriculum be of a high standard? For vocational subjects, will it be immediately relevant to the student's subsequent safe and effective entry into professional or other training? Will it be generally respected by employers as relevant to their needs?

- Will the award of a degree by an institution be respected or has it been subject to grade inflation or compromised by cheating at examinations?

Some of the information that is required to answer the above questions can be accessed readily, some will require tenacious enquiry, and some will be difficult to obtain. Yet all remain important for future educational and professional success.

A common error is to focus first on a university and hope that the subject and course will be satisfactory. In recent years the head teachers of independent schools have suggested that students needed to be more careful with their applications. Instead of focusing on trendy or fashionable universities with 'peer group reputation' or 'transient popularity', students should seek out highly rated departments at less popular universities.[2] The northern universities of Newcastle, Durham, Leeds, Liverpool, Manchester, Sheffield and York are positioning themselves as the 'N8' group to challenge the supremacy of Oxbridge, Imperial College and University College London. According to Brian Cantor, vice-chancellor of York: 'There is a certain degree of excessive self-confidence about the golden triangle. I came from Oxford and I'm not against concentration and selectivity. But it is an unarguable case that the country can't develop the way it wants based upon just the South-East or just three universities.' Alan Gilbert, president of the merged Manchester University, claimed: 'We are not far short of matching these [golden triangle] institutions in terms of our research and research culture.'[3] But these universities are moulding their reputations around strengths in research and, as we have seen, the relevance of institutional research to teaching is unproven or may even be harmful (see Chapter 5). This was not what the head teachers of independent schools were arguing for. They were emphasising the importance of first identifying the highly rated departments; the university is of secondary consideration.

So, the first goal is to identify the subject, and then to choose the course that best suits a student's personal learning style. There are substantial differences in how universities approach teaching. In some, students may engage heavily in self-directed learning or working with their undergraduate colleagues in problem-based learning; they may only see a tutor infrequently. Other courses may provide substantially more taught provision. An appropriate choice of course is vital.

Using this approach may narrow the choice considerably... or not. A student wishing to study auctioneering or Sinhalese will have no difficulty in deciding on a course or university: there is a choice of one. Prospective students of osteopathy have half a dozen or so courses to choose from, and veterinary science about twice as many. But with many other subjects, such as politics, psychology and the sciences, the choice increases dramatically: molecular biology alone is offered on 175 courses at over 50 universities, while law in various guises is covered by over 1,500 courses, many of which will fulfil the teaching-style criterion. So, there can remain formidable difficulties in weighing up choices. But the real challenge is not in finding data but whether the available information is reliable or not.

The various newspaper 'good university guides' and websites afford a useful introduction but, as we saw in Chapter 3, need to be interpreted with caution. A league table consulted in conjunction with the latest National Student Survey and the Teaching Quality Information website (see Appendix 1) may be a helpful combination.

Prospectuses and universities' own websites remain a main recruiting mechanism for universities wishing to sell their wares. These will probably contain most of what a student needs to know regarding entry requirements, course details, facilities and general information about the university, the city and surrounding areas. Remember, however, that they are written to sell a product and crafted by skilled marketing departments. Indeed, competition for students and research support has ensured that many universities have focused on image and corporate identity. Statements such as 'the university is committed to achieving excellence in teaching and research', 'we maintain a learning environment of the highest quality', 'our teaching and research is amongst the best in UK' are at best vague, and the first part of this book will, I hope, have alerted students to question what is actually meant by them. For example, prospective students should endeavour to find out as much hard information as possible about:

- whether epithets such as 'best' or 'excellent' refer to teaching, or simply reflect a grading in the Research Assessment Exercise (see chapter 5);
- the actual expected student–staff ratio for the course in which they are interested (see Chapter 6) and how it compares with the range of values elsewhere.

Appendix 1 gives a short list of websites that can provide a starting point.

A personal visit to a university can be instructive. Universities will be presenting their best face on open days, but talking to academic staff and particularly the current students can usually provide a clearer insight into the pros and cons of living and working in that environment. Appendix 3 suggests some further questions that students may like to ask. The views of final-year students and recent graduates provide a particularly important perspective on the quality and value of a course and degree. Those who have up-to-date, first-hand experience could help improve the information at present available to prospective students, parents, family and friends, career advisers, and admissions and academic staff. Many battles remain to be fought!

Conclusion

Conclusion

UNIVERSITIES ARE A national 'institution' and, as with any such institution, reputations and performance are frequently perceived to be what we prefer to believe to be true. Such perceptions inevitably involve elements of deception, myth and magic. Those within an institution are expected to embrace and defend its culture; they become 'institutionalised'. To challenge the culture from within can result in exclusion. Ivan Illich, the famous and vitriolic critic of schooling, might suggest an ethical awakening and that we move from inherited myth to respected procedure.[1]

Over the last decade the weekly deluge of articles on education in the national press has revealed our society's insatiable interest in all aspects of education. Higher education and its lack of financial support is well accepted. In a survey of public opinion in 2003, between 93 and 95 per cent of people from all political parties disagreed with the statement: 'They [universities] probably don't really need more money.'[2] The universities' attempts to harness and direct this support were ineffectual or absent. Educational fatigue reflects exhaustion in the face of dreary political rhetoric and bureaucratic insult.

This book has summarised some of the important challenges facing universities: the pressures caused by the dramatic increase in student numbers and decline in resources; the changing standards of the increased student intake; the difficulties of attracting students from less privileged backgrounds; the diverse requirements of the various stakeholders in higher education; the serious tensions between research and teaching and the problematic consequences for some universities in prioritising research and, in so doing raising questions over the standard of undergraduate education. There are additional problems resulting from universities attempting to attract students based on the promise of better jobs and better paid jobs, when the evidence to support such views is seriously questioned. Many of these issues relate to another, profound issue: the compromising of universities as institutions of truth and integrity.

Higher education is likely to remain at the top of the social agenda as the pressures increase. Success at university is now perceived to be the gateway to establishing a foothold in life. However, in September 2007 alone it was reported that:

- According to tutoring agencies, undergraduates are increasingly turning to private tutors, amid concerns that they are ill prepared for higher education and are not getting enough support from their universities![3] This built on a Higher Education Policy Institute (HEPI) survey of students' experiences and expectations in higher education in the UK that found a 'huge disparity' between the teaching hours offered in different subjects.[4]

- An HEPI survey of undergraduate student workload in Europe reported that UK students are getting fewer hours of tuition than those in Europe, which occasioned a lively debate with respect to 'value for money' in the UK.[5]

- For the first time in the UK a private, profit-making company has been given the power to award degrees, and this has created further tension.[6]

- A survey by HEPI revealed a 'worrying' 27 per cent of international students believed they received 'poor' or 'very poor' value for money. However, a survey by the International Graduate Insight Group, commissioned by the Council for Industry and Higher Education, reported that UK universities are the best in the world for teaching and supporting their international students.[7]

It will be interesting to see if 'September '07' becomes the nadir in the annals of higher education.

Yet the Government continues to create uncertainty in the funding of research with plans to award research grants according to criteria relating to their 'economic impact'. The disadvantages of this in terms of attempting such measurements have been well-rehearsed.[8] In particular Sir Howard Newby has stressed the wider social and cultural importance of academic institutions: 'There is more to higher education than a core function of contributing to economic growth... The defence of reason, the cultivation of young minds and the extension of a civilising influence are not the kinds of concepts that pass the test of Treasury scrutiny in spending reviews. Nevertheless, that is no reason why we in the higher education world should abandon them.'[9]

But generally the plight of young researchers in attempting to gain their own grant support has been ignored. Grave difficulties now face our younger colleagues in obtaining research funding and an academic post to secure a base to develop their academic careers – and the future of higher education. The vice-chancellor of Cambridge University is surely correct in concluding that the issue is 'undoubtedly important for the long-term economic health of this country'.[10] A further problem is that nowhere do the new research funding arrangements focus on the need to support research relevant to teaching needs and, in particular, to support the teaching–research nexus.

But it is within the remit of higher education to address the self-induced harm to reputation in the prioritising of research over teaching, the questionable degree classifications and the lessening respect for the credentialing process. Students and their parents, together with other stakeholders, particularly employers, should contribute to the discussions. There appears also to be some good news for students. In October Lord Triesman, the higher education minister, was given the new title of 'Minister for Students'. The creation of a new student forum was announced that would keep ministers informed as to 'what it is that students in the modern world may want'.[11]

There are numerous further issues and opinions to be shared, particularly those which may differ from the views expressed in this book. To this end, the creation of a website is a logical outcome, to explore the additional evidence. Readers of this book and others are invited to contribute (www.whosedegree. co.uk).

Appendices

Appendix 1: Useful Sources of Information

Universities and Colleges Admission Service (www.ucas.com/search) allows you to search by specific course subjects, entry qualifications, contact details etc. UCAS also produces a range of printed publications.

www.ukcoursefinder.com allows you to search for a course by subject or university and also has some advice and further links on choosing and applying.

www.hotcourses.com can be used to search and apply for courses, but its most useful component is its recent 'reviews' of specific courses by students themselves.

Aim Higher (www.aimhigher.ac.uk) has a particular focus on reaching families and communities who do not have a tradition of entering higher education and provides all necessary information on choosing a course, selecting a college or university, dealing with funding issues and so on.

HERO (www.hero.ac.uk) provides links to all UK universities and colleges that provide higher education, and advice on choosing and applying.

www.dfes.gov.uk/recognisedukdegrees provides information on institutions offering bona fide UK degrees and a warning about 'bogus' degrees.

The government portal **www.dfes.gov.uk/hegateway** provides links to organisations involved in higher education, including HEFCE, HESA, UCAS and teaching and student associations.

The **Teaching Quality Information** website (www1.tqi.ac.uk) has a facility that allows students to select and compare their own choice of universities related to an expected tariff point score, together with a worked example.

Psychometric testing

Psychometrics, the science of personality assessment for job opportunities, has been practised for decades in the USA. Many Americans know their Myers-Briggs designations off by heart. The reliability of the tests is open to debate and Langley provides a useful and accessible review of the tests.[1] But in the recruitment process for jobs, psychometric testing is used mainly to affirm that the character and aptitude of the applicant is right for the vacant position. There are numerous excellent websites offering practical help and advice, including www.vnunet.com/features/1154710 and www.vnunet.com/features/1154711.

It is helpful to know that Professor Glenn Ellenbogen, a New York psychologist, once profiled the personality of a corpse. Since the test gave credit for non-responses, he discovered that it had an IQ of 45 and was likely to enjoy reasonable popularity around the office.[2]

Appendix 2: The Russell Group of Universities

Birmingham
Bristol
Cambridge
Cardiff
Edinburgh
Glasgow
Imperial College of Science, Technology and Medicine
King's College London
Leeds
Liverpool
London School of Economics and Political Science
Manchester
Newcastle upon Tyne
Nottingham
Oxford
Queen's University Belfast
Sheffield
Southampton
University College London
Warwick

Appendix 3: Some Questions to Ask

A questionnaire to help parents and prospective students assess the quality of undergraduate education

The most troubling aspects of higher education with regard to the undergraduate experience relate to a lack of honesty or integrity by the university. Some students and parents perceive that there have been attempts by some universities:

- to legally constrain the already limited legal rights of students; and

- to subordinate teaching to research.

The task of prospective students and their parents is to identify the universities that provide the most satisfying undergraduate experience and best help the student to learn most, both academically and socially. Quality undergraduate instruction is paramount and may in the first instance be revealed in attempts:

- not to reduce the academic staff contact hours for undergraduate student teaching;

- not to reduce the scheduled hours for undergraduate teaching;

- not to increase unnecessarily the hourage for undergraduate 'student self-directed/self-centred learning';

- not to substitute part-time teaching staff, research assistants or postgraduate students for experienced academic staff;

- not to reduce staff-intensive tutorial groups and laboratory classes; and

- not to pack as many students as possible into large lecture theatres.

Questions can be designed to provide an initial insight into the character of an institution, its honesty and integrity, and into the quality of the undergraduate experience. The following questions can be addressed, as appropriate, to members of the institution: the vice-chancellor, rector, principal, head of department/section (HOD), the academic and administrative staff, and/or undergraduate students. One is looking for a consistent response from different groups to aid students and parents in their choice of university. An additional bonus, if students and their parents ask such questions, is that universities may improve the quality of their undergraduate provision.

Q1. Dear Vice-Chancellor/Principal/Rector: Have you led your university in an attempt to restrict the legal rights of undergraduate students in the event of the university failing to provide satisfactory standards in the provision of teaching and learning?

Q2. Dear Vice-Chancellor/Principal/Rector: In America parents and students receive literature about campus affairs, invitations to receptions with the university president and controlled access to academic staff, and to officials, to address their concerns. Do such activities exist or are you planning for similar arrangements within your own university?

Q3. Dear HOD: What were the results from the recent undergraduate National Student Surveys for course X and for the university?

Q4. Dear HOD: How many weeks in the academic year are devoted to actual contact teaching between the academic staff and students (as distinct from reading weeks, holidays, examinations and assessments) on the chosen course?

Q5. Dear HOD: What are the average contact hours per week for first, second, third and further years of teaching between the academic staff and students on the chosen course?

Q6. Dear students: Is the teaching between students and academic staff on the chosen course undertaken on Mondays and Fridays?

Q7. Dear HOD: What proportion of students on course X passed their examinations last year at the first attempt in the first, second, third, fourth years of study?

Q8. Dear HOD: Does the university or department have any established mechanism for taking into account the disparity in working hours spent in paid employment/commuting between undergraduate students, with respect to examination marking or undergraduate degree rankings?

Q9. Dear HOD: Has the university prioritised research over teaching in its overall goals?

Q10. Dear HOD/academic staff: Are academic staff promoted primarily on the basis of achievements in research?

Q11. Dear HOD/academic staff: Are academic staff promoted primarily on the basis of achievements in undergraduate teaching?

Q12. Dear HOD/academic staff: Are academic staff promoted primarily on the basis of achievements in research and administrative responsibilities?

Q13. Dear HOD/academic staff: Are professors appointed primarily on the basis of achievements in research?

Q14. Dear HOD/academic staff: If professors have been appointed primarily on the basis of achievements in research, has the appointment been made to enhance an existing research group or to strengthen the teaching–research nexus?

Q15. Dear HOD/academic staff: Have any professors been appointed primarily on the basis of achievements in teaching?

Q16. Dear HOD/academic staff: Are professors appointed on the basis of achievements in administration or management?

Q17. Dear HOD/academic staff: What proportion of academic staff appointments been made primarily on the basis of achievements in research in the last five years?

Q18. Dear HOD/academic staff: What proportion and how many academic staff appointments have been made primarily on the basis of achievements in teaching expertise in the last five years?

Q19. Dear HOD/academic staff: What proportion of the staff–student contact hours is undertaken by professors teaching undergraduate students?

Q20. Dear HOD/academic staff: What are the average contact-hours per year for professorial staff in formal contact teaching time with undergraduate students?

Q21. Dear HOD/academic staff: Are academic staff who undertake research with no teaching responsibilities paid from undergraduate student fees?

Q22. Dear HOD/academic staff: What is the student:staff ratio for the department?

Q23. Dear HOD/academic staff: Within the last five-year period, has small group/seminar/tutorial teaching been reduced?

Q24. Dear HOD/academic staff: Within the last five-year period, has small group/seminar/tutorial teaching been increased?

Q25. Dear HOD/academic staff: Within the last five-year period, if the department has lost identity or been coalesced into a larger administrative unit, what effective steps, if any, have been taken to provide students and academic staff with a group identity?

Q26. Dear HOD/academic staff: Do you perceive that the academic staff do their best to provide academic or personal support for students in addition to their scheduled teaching commitments?

Q27. Dear students: Do you perceive that the academic staff do their best to provide you with academic or personal support in addition to their scheduled teaching commitments?

Q28. Dear students: Given the overall pressures on academic staff to fulfil their teaching, research or administrative duties, do you believe that the teaching of undergraduate students is maintained at an acceptable level?

Q29. Dear students: Do you, a first-year student, consider that attending the university has been an enjoyable and rewarding experience, and how would you rate it on a satisfaction scale of 0 to 5?

Q30. Dear students: What do you, a final-year student, consider the most significant features of the present course and university, and how would you rate the course and university on a satisfaction scale of 0 to 5?

Q31. Dear students: What do you, a final-year student, consider the most significant failings of the present course and university?

Q32. Dear Vice-Chancellor/HOD: Is the department or university seeking to identify the successes and limitations of the undergraduate courses through consultation with the employers of its students?

Q30. Dear Vice-Chancellor/HOD: Is the department or university seeking to identify the successes and limitations of the undergraduate courses through consultation with its graduate students?

For some courses and universities it may be important to establish the A-level entry grades of the students: student peer-group interactions are an important factor in student learning.

Notes

Notes

Introduction

1   Macleod, D. (2003) 'Mapping the future', *Guardian Education*, 18 March.

Chapter 1 Higher education: a global industry

1   Newman, J.H. (1959) *The idea of a university* (New York: Doubleday), pp. 192, 144–5.
2   Soffer, R.N. (1994) *Discipline and power: the university, history, and the making of an English elite, 1870–1930* (Stanford University Press), p. 20.
3   Blunkett, Rt Hon. D. (2000) *Modernising higher education – facing the global challenge* (speech delivered at the University of Greenwich, 15 February) (London: Department for Education and Employment).
4   Leadbeater, C. (1999) *Living on thin air: the new economy* (London: Penguin).
5   Blair, T. (1999) *The learning habit* (Romanes Lecture delivered by the Prime Minister at Oxford University, 2 December), available on the 10 Downing Street website: http://www.number-10.gov.uk/news.asp?NewsId=4168&SectionId=32
6   Confederation of British Industry (1994) *Thinking ahead: ensuring the expansion of higher education into the 21st century* (London: CBI).
7   news.bbc.co.uk/1/hi/education/569044.stm, 24 December 1999.
8   Ryan, A. (2005) 'A possibility is that a degree is used by employers as an easy way to draw a line between the folk they are willing to employ and those they are not', *Times Higher Education Supplement*, 28 January.
9   Denison, E.F. (1962) *The sources of economic growth in the United States and the alternatives before us* (New York: Committee on Economic Development). Schultz, T. (1962) 'Reflections on investment in human beings', *Journal of Political Economy*, 10, Supplement, October, pp. 1–8. Bowman, M.J. (1966) 'The human investment revolution in economic thought', *Sociology of Education*, 39, pp. 111–37.
10   Harris, S. (1949) *The market for college graduates* (Harvard University Press), p. 64. See also Berg, I. (1970) *Education and jobs: the great training robbery* (New York: Praeger), pp. 186–90.
11   Hutchins, R.M. (1964) *The University of Utopia* (Charles R. Walgreen Foundation Lectures) (Chicago: University of Chicago Press).
12   Berg, I. (1970) *Education and jobs: the great training robbery* (New York: Praeger), pp. 1–15.
13   Ibid., p. 11.

Chapter 2 The corporatisation of universities

1 Kadish, A. (1986) *Apostle Arnold: the life and death of Arnold Toynbee 1852–1883* (Durham, NC: Duke University Press), pp. 177, 231–2.
2 Chapman, J.J. (1909) 'The Harvard Classics and Harvard', *Science*, 30, p. 440.
3 Flexnor, A. (1930) *Universities, American, English, German* (New York: Oxford University Press), p. 154.
4 Caws, P. (1970) 'Design for a university', *Daedalus*, Winter, p. 98.
5 Aronowitz, S. (2000) *The knowledge factory: dismantling the corporate university and creating true higher learning* (Boston: Beacon Press), p. 164.
6 Brown, A.R., Gaskell, M., and Eggins, H. (2004) *Higher education and the public good* (London: Society for Research into Higher Education, The Council for Industry and Higher Education).
7 Veblen, T. (1918) *The higher learning in America: a memorandum on the conduct of universities by business men* (New York: Sagamore Press, reprint 1957), p. 209.
8 Bok, D. (2003) *Universities in the marketplace: the commercialization of higher education* (Princeton and Oxford: Princeton University Press), pp. 24, 30.
9 Ibid.
10 Ibid., pp. 26, 29.
11 Ibid., pp. 18, 19.
12 Bundy, C. (2004) 'We'd like to be America', *Times Higher Education Supplement*, 9 July. Bok, D. (2003) *Universities in the marketplace: the commercialization of higher education* (Princeton and Oxford: Princeton University Press), pp. 32–3.
13 Bok, D. (2003) *Universities in the marketplace: the commercialization of higher education* (Princeton and Oxford: Princeton University Press), p. 35.
14 Mayer, M. (1993) *Robert Maynard Hutchins: a memoir* (Berkeley: University of California Press).
15 Bok, D. (2003) *Universities in the marketplace: the commercialization of higher education* (Princeton and Oxford: Princeton University Press), pp. 125–9.
16 Ibid., pp. 41–6.
17 Ibid., p. 107.
18 Boyer, E.L. (1987) *College: the undergraduate experience in America*, The Carnegie Foundation for the Advancement of Teaching (San Francisco: Jossey-Bass), p. 184.
19 Duderstadt, J.J. (2000) *Intercollegiate athletics and the American University: a university president's perspective* (University of Michigan Press), p. 201.
20 Quoted in the Knight Commission on Intercollegiate Athletics (2001), *A call to action: reconnecting college sports and higher education* (The Knight Commission), p. 8 (www. knightcommission.org).
21 Bok, D. (2003) *Universities in the marketplace: the commercialization of higher education* (Princeton and Oxford: Princeton University Press), pp. 46–51.
22 Waters, L. (2004) *Enemies of promise: publishing, perishing and the eclipse of scholarship* (Chicago: Prickly Paradigm Press), p. 6.
23 Baty, P. (2006) 'Academia has sold out, 72% believe', *Times Higher Education Supplement*, 27 October.
24 Baty, P. (2006) 'Profs attack managers', *Times Higher Education Supplement*, 24 November.
25 Marginson, S. and Considine, M. (2001) *The enterprise university: power, governance and reinvention in Australia* (Cambridge University Press), p. 11.

26 Baty, P. and Sanders, C. (2006) 'Leeds housing win prompts call for fight against "unfair" contracts', *Times Higher Education Supplement*, 22 September.

27 Fazackerley, A. (2006) 'Student anger as Reading drops physics', *Times Higher Education Supplement*, 6 October, p. 4.

28 Sapstead, D. and Highfield, R. (2004) 'Students fight to save architecture department at Cambridge', *Daily Telegraph*, 30 November.

29 Tysome, T. (2004) 'Oxford bid to halve tutorials is slated', *Times Higher Education Supplement*, 5 November.

30 Fazackerley, A. (2004) 'Furious parents round on Exeter', *Times Higher Education Supplement*, 17 December.

31 Lipsett, A. (2006) '13% misled by brochure', *Times Higher Education Supplement*, 2 November.

32 Tysome, T. (2006) 'Young guns ditch old values', *Times Higher Education Supplement*, 15 December.

33 Tysome, T. (2000) 'Charities fume over tobacco funding', *Times Higher Education Supplement*, 8 December. Tysome, T. (2001) 'Editor calls for a tobacco-funding debate', *Times Higher Education Supplement*, 7 July.

34 Fazackerley, A. and Tysome, T. (2004) 'Row rages over dirty money', *Times Higher Education Supplement*, 27 May.

35 Tysome, T., Johnston, C. and Wojtas, O. (2004) 'Elite stump up millions in hunt for research stars', *Times Higher Education Supplement*, 7 July.

36 Baty, P. (2004) 'Trent shake-up follows staff poll', *Times Higher Education Supplement*, 9 July.

37 Kirp, D. (2004) 'No place for losers', *Times Higher Education Supplement*, 9 April.

Chapter 3 Student selection: do bias and prejudice exist?

1 Goddard, A. (2005) 'LSE sets secret state quota', *Times Higher Education Supplement*, 11 March.

2 Scott-Clark, C., Driscoll, M. and Steiner, R. (1996) 'Privilege and prejudice', *Sunday Times*, 7 July.

3 Ibid.

4 Ibid.

5 O'Reilly, J. and Byrne, C. (1997) 'Universities shun Eton's high-fliers', *Sunday Times*, 29 June.

6 Clare, J. (1999) 'Oxford bias against state pupils "starts at interview"', *Daily Telegraph*, 10 November.

7 The Sutton Trust (2000) *Entry to leading universities*, http://www.suttontrust.com/reports/entryToLeadingUnis.pdf

8 Ibid.

9 O'Reilly, J. (1998) 'Comprehensives intake at Oxbridge under 20%', *Sunday Times*, 11 January.

10 Cunningham, V. (2000) 'Prejudice, yes; at Oxford, no', *Times Higher Education Supplement*, 9 June.

11 Elliott, J. and Hackett, G. (2004) 'Oxford admissions reveal bias to state pupils', *Sunday Times*, 5 December.

12 Hackett, G. (2006) 'Poorer pupils still fail to get into Oxbridge', *Sunday Times*, 17 December.

13 Grimston, J. and Dobson, R. (2002) 'So which one is privileged?', *Sunday Times*.
14 Halpin, T. (2003) 'Universities "must show they are open to all"', *The Times*, 9 April.
15 O'Leary, J. (1999) 'Bristol breaks ranks to offer a leg-up for deprived students', *The Times*, 14 September.
16 O'Leary, J. (1999) 'University moves to broaden social mix', *The Times*, 14 September.
17 Owen, G. (2002) 'Private schools to meet universities over bias claims', *The Times*, 21 December.
18 Haplin, T. (2003) 'Universities urged to use blind selection', *The Times*, 11 April.
19 Henry, J. (2003) 'Good A-level grades are no longer enough as leading colleges give preference to local students', *Sunday Telegraph*, 9 September.
20 Glover, S. (2002) 'A monstrous betrayal of ALL children', *Daily Mail*, 5 November.
21 Adamson, J. (2003) 'We dons are being asked to destroy what we hold most dear', *Sunday Telegraph*, 9 March.
22 Henry, J. (2004) 'Oxford university admits it at last: it does discriminate against students from independent schools', *Sunday Telegraph*, 5 December.
23 Witheridge, J. (2007) 'Our exam system will soon prove calamitous', sundaytelegraph.co.uk, 25 August.
24 *Hansard*, 13 March 2003.
25 Marston, P. (1994) 'New angle on results', *The Times*, 1 August.
26 Ibid.
27 Abrams, F. (2003) 'Living in the never-never land?', *Times Educational Supplement*, 3 October.
28 Naylor, R. and Smith, J. (2002) *Schooling effects on subsequent university performance: evidence for the UK university population*, **Warwick Economic Research Papers**, no. 657 (University of Warwick, Dept. of Economics).
29 Owen, G. (2002) 'School fees won't buy a good degree', *The Times*, 7 December.
30 Thomson, A. and Goddard, A. (2003) 'Let state pupils in on lower A levels', *Times Higher Education Supplement*, 23 January.
31 'New friends in the North', *The Guardian*, 4 February 2003.
32 Hackett, G. (2006) 'Poorer pupils still fail to get into Oxbridge', *Sunday Times*, 17 December.
33 Thomas, E. (2004) 'Opinion: Those bright young people who do not get into Oxbridge are hardly "rejects"', *The Guardian*, 20 January.
34 Goddard, A. (2004) 'Trainee medics are top of "posh" league', *Times Higher Education Supplement*, 30 April. Goddard, A. (2004) 'Subjects slot into class divide', *Times Higher Education Supplement*, 30 April.
35 Hill, P. (2005) 'The high-flyers who don't stray far from the nest', *Times Higher Education Supplement*, Section Access: Widening participation in higher education, 21 January. Higher Education Funding Council (2005) *Young participation in higher education* (Bristol: HEFCE). See also Archer, L., Hutchings, M. and Ross, A. (2003) *Higher education and social class: issues of exclusion and inclusion* (London: RoutledgeFalmer); and Reay, D. and Ball, S.J. (1997) 'Spoilt for choice: the working classes and education markets', *Oxford Review of Education*, 14(1), 57–75.
36 Halpin, T. (2003) 'Most students regret their A-level choices', *The Times*, 13 November.
37 Halpin, T. and Owen, G. (2003) 'Pass rate soars as pupils chase "easy" A levels', *The Times*, 14 August.

38 Frean, A. (2007) 'Success, or a study in failure? Blair's school conundrum', *The Times*, 4 May. Garner, R. (2007) 'A new legacy for Blair: study reveals record numbers of children sent to independent schools', *The Independent*, 4 May.
39 Meikle, J. (2007) 'State pupils still struggle to access top universities', educationguardian.co.uk, 19 July. Tysome, T. (2007) 'Access agenda is now back on track', *Times Higher Education Supplement*, 20 July.

Chapter 4 The league tables minefield

1   Wright, D. (2003) 'Patients misled, says BMA chairman', *The Times*, 14 July.
2   Halpin, T. (2005) 'State schools top the table but private rivals cry foul', *The Times*, 13 January.
3   O'Leary, J. (2003) 'How ratings rank', *The Times*, The Times Good University Guide, 7 May.
4   Marcus, J. (2007) 'US rankings opponents struggling to turn tables', *Times Higher Education Supplement*, 22 June.
5   Marcus, J. (2007) 'Nutty idea that might catch on? Campus squirrel ranking puts Berkeley in the lead', *Times Higher Education Supplement*, 22 June. The amusing Campus Squirrel Listings are featured in many US university publications (www.gotshall.com/squirrels/campsq.htm).
6   Marcus, J. (2007) 'US rankings opponents struggling to turn tables', *Times Higher Education Supplement*, 22 June.
7   [Editorial] (2007) 'Rank and defile', *Times Higher Education Supplement*, 22 June.
8   Bok, D. (2003) *Universities in the market place; the commercialization of higher education* (Princeton University Press), pp. 160–62.
9   Kirp, D. (2004) *Shakespeare, Einstein, and the bottom line; the marketing of higher education* (Cambridge, MA: Harvard University Press), pp. 25–6.
10 See www.usnews.com/usnews/edu/college/rankings/about/weight_brief.php
11 Stecklow, S. (1995) 'Colleges inflate SATs and graduation rates in popular guidebooks', *Wall Street Journal*, 5 April.
12 Fazackerley, A. and Shepherd, J. (2005) 'Student poll puts staff under pressure', *Times Higher Education Supplement*, 23 September.
13 Ibid.
14 Ibid.
15 Shepherd, J. (2005) 'I could be online with my class while in my bunker', *Times Higher Education Supplement*, 23 September.
16 McCall, A. (2005) 'Building a picture of a happy body of students', *Sunday Times*, University Guide, 2 October.
17 McCall, A. (2005) 'Heads turn tables', *Sunday Times*, University Guide, 2 October.
18 Fazackerley. A. (2005) 'Redbricks get thumbs down, *Times Higher Education Supplement*, 23 September.
19 Attwood, R. and Radnofsky, L. (2007) 'Satisfied – but students want more feedback', *Times Higher Education Supplement*, 14 September.

Chapter 5 The research effect

1   Newman, J.H. (1959) *The idea of a university* (New York: Doubleday), pp. 192, 144–5.

2   Bok, D. (2006) *Our underachieving colleges: a candid look at how much students learn and why they should be learning more* (Princeton University Press), pp. 1–10.

3   [Editorial] (2001) 'Academic interest: universities need to be relieved from destructive research rules', *The Times*, 1 May.

4   Fazackerley, A. (2003) 'May doubts research link', *Times Higher Education Supplement*, 5 December.

5   Macleod, D. (2003) 'Mapping the future', *Guardian Education*, 18 March.

6   Kroto, H. (2003) 'Chemists should remove scientific inventions from the lives of those such as Billy Connolly and Jeremy Clarkson who rubbish science education', *Times Higher Education Supplement*, 18 April.

7   Higher Education Council (1992) *Higher education: achieving quality* (Canberra: Australian Government Publishing Service).

8   Drennan, L.T. and Beck, M. (2000) 'Teaching quality performance indicators: key influences on the UK universities' acute scores', *Quality Assurance in Education*, 9, pp. 92–102.

9   House of Commons Education and Skills Committee (2003) *The Future of Higher Education*. Fifth Report of Session 2002–2003. Volume 1. Report and formal minutes. HC 425–1, p. 14.

10 Baty, P. (2003) 'Sykes says teaching-only sites will be second-rate institutions', *Times Higher Education Supplement*, 14 March.

11 Newman, M. (2007) 'Centres of excellence fail to transform teaching', *Times Higher Education Supplement*, 13 July.

12 Pascarella, E.T. and Terenzini, P.T. (1991) *How college affects students* (San Francisco: Jossey-Bass). Terenzini, P.T. and Pascarella, E.T. (1994) 'Living with myths: undergraduate education in America', *Change*, 27(5), pp. 45–9. Ramsden, P. and Moses, I. (1992) 'Association between research and teaching in Australian higher education', *Higher Education*, 23(3), pp. 273–95.

13 Astin, A.W. (1993) *What matters in college? Four critical years revisited* (San Francisco: Jossey-Bass).

14 Astin, A.W. and Chang, M.J. (1995) 'Colleges that emphasise research and teaching: can you have your cake and eat it too?', *Change*, 27(5), pp. 44–9.

15 Gibbs, G. (1995) 'The relationship between quality in research and quality in teaching', *Quality in Higher Education*, 1(2), pp. 147–57.

16 Neumann, R. (1994) 'The teaching–research nexus: applying a framework to university students' learning experiences', *European Journal of Education*, 29(3), pp. 323–38.

17 Boyer, E.L. (1987) *College: the undergraduate experience in America*, The Carnegie Foundation for the Advancement of Teaching (San Francisco: Jossey-Bass), pp. 127–31.

18 Jenkins, A., Breen, R. and Lindsay, R. (2003) *Reshaping teaching in higher education: linking teaching with research* (Birmingham: Seda/Kogan Page), pp. 1–29.

19 Astin, A.W. (1993) *What matters in college? Four critical years revisited* (San Francisco: Jossey-Bass), pp. 410–12.

20 House of Commons Education and Skills Committee (2003) *The Future of Higher Education*. Fifth Report of Session 2002–2003. Volume 1. Report and formal minutes. HC 425–1, p. 20.

21 Ibid., p.3.
22 Utley, A. (1997) 'Teaching in decline, says study', *Times Higher Education Supplement*, 18 April.
23 Leon, P. (2002) 'Research strategy limits teaching of students', *Times Higher Education Supplement*, 18 July.
24 Dorey, P. (2003) Letter to the editor, *The Times*, 3 June.
25 Fazackerley, A. (2005) 'King's to cut life sciences', *Times Higher Education Supplement*, 5 December.
26 Owen, G., (2003) 'Oxford's superiority over "poly" is history', *The Times*, 20 June.
27 Dorrell, E. (2003) 'Cambridge's decision to axe its architecture course proves the discipline is under threat', *Guardian Education*, 29 July.
28 Utley, A. (2004) 'Lancaster to axe art to focus on music', *Times Higher Education Supplement*, 11 June.
29 Thomson, A. (2004) 'Aberdeen to axe 80 staff', *Times Higher Education Supplement*, 11 June.
30 Owen, G. (2003) 'Oxford's superiority over "poly" is history', *The Times*, 20 June.
31 Lewis, J. (2003) 'Why I think the RAE review needs to go back to basics', *Times Higher Education Supplement*, 10 January.
32 Fazackerley, A. (2003) 'MPs criticise Nerc's grant cancellation', *Times Higher Education Supplement*, 25 July. McDowell, N. (2002) 'Top projects suffer as medical funding falters', *Nature*, 418, p. 714.
33 Goddard, A. (2003) 'RAE chairs: "We'll pull out"', *Times Higher Education Supplement*, 2 May.
34 Davis, C. (2003) 'Fear silenced grant protests', *Times Higher Education Supplement*, 28 March.
35 Tysome, T. (2007) 'Opinions', *Times Higher Education Supplement*, 1 June.
36 Goddard, A. (2003) 'Revamped RAE to start a year early', *Times Higher Education Supplement*, 18 April.
37 Fazackerley, A. (2003) 'End RAE, demands Royal Society', *Times Higher Education Supplement*, 16 May.
38 Colquhoun, D. (2007) 'Imperial College London's performance measures', *Times Higher Education Supplement*, 1 June.
39 Goddard, A. (2003) 'UUK: no evidence to back research focus', *Times Higher Education Supplement*, 24 October.
40 Owen, G. (2003) 'Elite university funding "will hit jobs and research"', *Times Higher Education Supplement*, 23 October.
41 Piper, M.P.A. (2001) President's address at the Board of Governors' retreat, University of British Columbia, www.vision.ubc.ca/supp_docs/piper_bog.html.

Chapter 6 Teaching, learning and earning: degrees of dilemma

1 Lipsett, A. (2005) 'Critics round on academy', *Times Higher Education Supplement*, 2 September.
2 Attwood, R. (2007) 'Teaching set for a big boost in promotions overhaul', *Times Higher Education Supplement*, 3 August.
3 Lipsett, A. (2006) 'Postdocs cover for teaching shortfall', *Times Higher Education Supplement*, 2 November.
4 Ibid.

5   Baty, P. (2006) 'Part-timers merit equality' and 'Call to use FoI to fight "abuse" by managers', *Times Higher Education Supplement,* 2 June.

6   Tysome, T. (2007) 'Dearing still shapes the agenda he set. Ten years on: Huge challenges remain', *Times Higher Education Supplement,* 27 July.

7   Newman, M. (2007) 'Class sizes spark fears over quality', *Times Higher Education Supplement,* 4 May.

8   Baty, P. (2006) 'QAA admits that students lose out', *Times Higher Education Supplement,* 9 November.

9   Baty, P. (2001) 'Russell elite go for jugular of ailing QAA', *Times Higher Education Supplement,* 21 September.

10 Arthgur, M. (2006) 'Student feedback acts as catalyst for positive change', *Sunday Times,* 10 September.

11 Baty, P. (2006) 'Overseas students given grade top ups at fashion college', *Times Higher Education Supplement,* 21 July.

12 Clark, L. (2006) 'Students can ask proof-readers to check their essays', *Times Higher Education Supplement,* 16 April.

13 Morrison, J. (2006) 'The cheats will never prosper', *The Independent,* 15 June.

14 Blair, A. (2005) 'Student work "rife with plagiarism"', *Times Higher Education Supplement,* 3 November.

15 Quoted in Mansell, W. and Ward, H. (2006) 'Explosion in cheating blamed on test culture', *Times Educational Supplement,* 19 May.

16 Aggarwal, R., Bates, I., Davies, J.G. and Khan, I. (2002) 'A study of academic dishonesty among students at two pharmacy schools', *Pharmaceutical Journal,* 269, 12 October, pp. 529–32.

17 Paton, G. (2006) 'Exams may be held in metal-lined rooms to stop cheats', *Times Higher Education Supplement,* 5 December.

18 Baty, P. (2006) 'Students still hazy on correct procedure', *Times Higher Education Supplement,* 23 June.

19 Shepherd, J. (2006) 'Staff not software will trap cheats', *Times Higher Education Supplement,* 19 May.

20 Attwood, R. (2007) 'Cheats: chaos in sanctions', *Times Higher Education Supplement,* 15 June.

21 Ibid.

22 Attwood, R. (2007) 'The bigger the bill, the greater the gripes', *Times Higher Education Supplement,* 17 August.

23 Baty, P. (2006) 'An academic's error has led to a fierce debate on what constitutes plagiarism; cheat experts in row over quote', *Times Higher Education Supplement,* 16 June.

24 Baty, P. (2006) 'Disarming fellow cheats death', *Times Higher Education Supplement,* 30 June.

25 Baty, P. (2006) 'Lecturer admits role in tutor firm', *Times Higher Education Supplement,* 20 October.

Chapter 7 How degrees are awarded

1   Baty, P. (2006) 'Grade system awarded "fail"', *Times Higher Education Supplement,* 29 September.

2   Lightfoot, L. (2006) 'Getting a first has become a lottery for brightest students', *Daily Telegraph,* 31 October.

3 Ibid.
4 Ibid.
5 Baty, P. (2006) 'Grade system awarded "fail"', *Times Higher Education Supplement*, 29 September.
6 Ibid.
7 Baty, P. (2006) 'New class proposed to end 2:1 bonanza', *Times Higher Education Supplement*, 9 November.
8 Ibid.
9 Ibid.

Chapter 8 The rights of students... or lack of them

1 Macfarlane, B. (2004) *Teaching with integrity: the ethics of higher education practice* (London: RoutledgeFalmer), p. 23.
2 *Donohue* v. *Copiague Union Free School District*. 391 N.E. 2d 1352,1353 (1979). Quoted in DeMitchell, T.A. and DeMitchell, T.A. (2003) 'Statutes and standards: has the door to educational malpractice been opened?', *B.Y.U. Education and Law Journal*, pp. 485, 498–9.
3 'Former V-C advocates superstore approach', *Times Higher Education Supplement*, 21 February 2003.
4 [Editorial] (2003) 'Unsatisfied students have no right to refund', *Times Higher Education Supplement*, 21 February.
5 Astin, A.W. (1993) *What matters in college? Four critical years revisited* (San Francisco: Jossey-Bass), pp. 17–23.
6 Evans, G.R. and Gill, J. (2001) *Universities and students: a guide to rights, responsibilities and practical remedies* (London: Kogan Page), pp. 136–7.
7 Ibid., p. 143.
8 Ibid., p. 137.
9 Ibid., pp. 137–41.
10 Evans, G.R. and Gill, J. (2001) *Universities and students; a guide to rights, responsibilities and practical remedies* (London: Kogan Page), pp. 148–9.
11 Baty, P. (2003) 'Student's human rights "were violated" claim', *Times Higher Education Supplement*, 16 May.
12 Baty, P. and Wainwright, T. (2005) 'Complaint culture grows on campus', *Times Higher Education Supplement*, 19 August.
13 Ibid.
14 Baty, P. and Wainwright, T. (2005) 'Lecture's off? I want my bus fare refunded', *Times Higher Education Supplement*, 19 August.
15 Based on the summary in Evans, G.R. and Gill, J. (2001) *Universities and students: a guide to rights, responsibilities and practical remedies* (London: Kogan Page), pp. 106–107.
16 Ibid., pp. 159–61.
17 Ibid., pp. 159–60.
18 Ibid., p. 149.
19 Baty, P. (2003) 'Aston faces £100,000 High Court claim', *Times Higher Education Supplement*, 7 March.
20 Baty, P., (2003) 'Student's human rights "were violated" claim', *Times Higher Education Supplement*, 16 May.

21 Sanders, C. (2003) 'UUK backs students' rights', *Times Higher Education Supplement*, 21 November.
22 Ibid.
23 Baty, P. (2004) 'Fear over legality of complaint watchdog', *Times Higher Education Supplement*, 26 March.
24 Ibid.
25 Ibid.
26 Baty, P. and Wainwright, T. (2005) 'Complaint culture grows on campus', *Times Higher Education Supplement*, 19 August.
27 Baty, P. and Wainwright, T. (2005) 'Lecture's off? I want my bus fare refunded', *Times Higher Education Supplement*, 19 August.
28 Baty, P. and Wainwright, T. (2005) 'Complaint culture grows on campus', *Times Higher Education Supplement*, 19 August.
29 Baty, P. and Wainwright, T. (2005) 'Lecture's off? I want my bus fare refunded', *Times Higher Education Supplement*, 19 August.
30 [Editorial] (2005) 'Customer care or collegiality', *Times Higher Education Supplement*, 19 August.
31 Newman, M. (2007) 'Move to curb student rights', *Times Higher Education Supplement*, 13 July.
32 Tysome, T. (2007) 'HEFCE aims to cut costly court bills', *Times Higher Education Supplement*, 9 February.

Chapter 9 Is higher education for all?

1 Brown, P., Hesketh. A. with Williams, S. (2004) *The mismanagement of talent: employability and jobs in the knowledge economy* (Oxford University Press), p. 1.
2 Hirsch, F. (1977) *The social limits to growth* (London: Routledge).
3 [Editorial] (2004) 'We don't want millions', *Yorkshire Post,* 6 November.
4 Blair, A. (2004) 'Rich list shows success at university of life', *The Times,* 17 June. See also *The Times,* 3 July 2007. *Sunday Times,* 29 April 2007.
5 Blair, A. (2004) 'Success at university of life pays off', *The Times,* 17 June.
6 Kasser, T. and Ryan, R.M. (1996) 'Further examining the American dream: different correlates of intrinsic and extrinsic goals', *Personality and Social Behaviour,* 22, pp. 280–87. Kasser, T. and Ryan, R.M. (2001) 'Be careful what you wish for: optimal functioning and the relative attainment of intrinsic and extrinsic goals', in Schmuck, P. and Sheldon, K.M. (eds) *Life goals and well-being: towards a positive psychology of human striving* (Cambridge, MA: Hogrefe & Huber). Sheldon, K.M. and Kasser, T. (1995) 'Coherence and congruence: two aspects of personality integration', *Journal of Personality and Social Psychology,* 68, pp. 531–43. Sheldon, K.M. and Kasser, T. (1998) 'Pursuing personal goals: skills enable progress, but not all progress is beneficial', *Personality and Social Bulletin,* 24, pp. 1319–31. Sheldon, K.M. and Kasser,T. (2001) '"Getting older, getting better": personal strivings and psychological maturity across the life span', *Development Psychology,* 37, pp. 491–501.
7 Saunders, S. and Munro, D. (2000) 'The construction and validation of a consumer orientation questionnaire (SCOI) designed to measure Fromm's (1955) "marketing character" in Australia', *Social Behaviour and Personality,* 28, pp. 219–40.
8 Chan, R. and Joseph, S.R. (2000) 'Dimensions of personality, domains of aspirations, and subjective well-being', *Personality and Individual Differences,* 28, pp. 347–54.

9   Schmuck, P., Kasser, T. and Ryan, R.M. (2000) 'Intrinsic and extrinsic goals: their structure and relationship to well-being in German and US college students', *Social Indicators Research*, 15, pp. 225–41.

10 Ryan, R.M., Chirkov, V.I., Little, T.D., Sheldon, K.M., Timoshina, E. and Deci, E.L. (1999) 'The American dream in Russia: extrinsic aspirations and well-being in two cultures', *Personality and Social Psychology Bulletin*, 25, pp.1509–24.

11 Kasser, T., Ahuvia, A.C. (2002) 'Materialistic values and well-being in business students', *European Journal of Social Psychology*, 32, pp.137–46.

12 Kasser, T., Ryan, R.M., Couchman, C.E. and Sheldon, K.M. (2003) 'Materialistic values: their causes and consequences', in Kasser, T. and Kanner, A.D. (eds) *Psychology and consumer culture: the struggle for a good life in a materialistic world* (Washington DC: American Psychological Association), p. 19.

13 Layard, R (2004) *Happiness: lessons from a new science* (London: Penguin), pp. 29–38.

14 Ryan, A. (2005) 'What's wrong is that economists have become the hired helpers of governments bent on making us all work long hours for no good reason', *Times Higher Education Supplement*, 25 February.

15 Chynoweth, C. (2005) 'Find your niche in life', *The Times*, Career section: Graduate Special, 13 January, p. 11.

16 [Editorial] (2004) 'We don't want millions', *Yorkshire Post*, 6 November.

17 Wolf, A. (2002) *Does education matter? Myths about education and economic growth* (London: Penguin), pp. 1–55. Harmon, C. and Walker, I. (1995) 'Estimates of the economic return to schooling for the United Kingdom', *American Economic Review*, 85, pp. 1278–85. Harmon, C. and Walker, I. (1999) 'The marginal and average return to schooling in the UK', *Economic Review*, 43, pp. 879–87.

18 Elliott, J. and Thomas, Z. (2003) 'Personality is the key to success in adult life', *Sunday Times*, 29 June.

19 Council for Industry and Higher Education (2003) *The Value of Higher Education*, October (www.Cihe-UK.com/publications.php)

20 Tysome, T. (2004) 'Graduate pay is on the up', *Times Higher Education Supplement*, 30 January.

21 Tysome, T. (2004) 'Graduates reap high returns degree', *Times Higher Education Supplement*, 17 September.

22 Jobbins, D. (2006) 'UK graduates reap salary rewards', *Times Higher Education Supplement*, 15 September.

23 Tysome, T. (2004) 'Employers toy with golden hellos to ease student debt', *Times Higher Education Supplement*, 23 January.

24 Chynoweth, C. (2005) 'Find your niche in life', *The Times Career: Graduate Special*, 13 January, p. 11.

25 *Sunday Times*, 2 September 2007.

26 Brown, P., Hesketh. A. with Williams, S. (2004) *The mismanagement of talent: employability and jobs in the knowledge economy* (Oxford University Press), p. 217.

Chapter 10 What are a student's prospects?

1   Lipsett, A. (2007) 'Firms turn to psychometric tests to pick graduate recruits', *Education Guardian*, 10 July.

2   Pryor, F.L. and Schaffer, D.L. (2000) *Who's not working and why? Employment, cognitive skills, wages and the changing U.S. Labor Market* (Cambridge University Press).

3 US Department of Labor (2001) *Office of the 21st century workforce* (Washington: US Department of Labor), p. 7.
4 Brown, P., Hesketh. A. with Williams, S. (2004) *The mismanagement of talent: employability and jobs in the knowledge economy* (Oxford University Press, p. 56.
5 Ibid., p. 63.
6 Smetherham, C. (2005) *A review of the literature on graduate employment, underemployment and unemployment* (Report for the independent study into the devolution of the student support system and tuition fee regime) (Cardiff University: School of Social Sciences), Briefing Paper 3, March.
7 Ibid., pp. 16–18, 44–5.
8 Berg, I. (1970) *Education and jobs: the great training robbery* (New York: Praeger), p. 81.
9 Keep, E. (2000) 'After access: researching labour market issues' in J. Gallacher (ed.) *Researching access to higher education* (London: Routledge). National Skills Task Force (2000) *Skills for all* (Sudbury: DfEE), p. 117. Brown, P., Hesketh. A. with Williams, S. (2004) *The mismanagement of talent: employability and jobs in the knowledge economy* (Oxford University Press), Chapter 3 'What knowledge economy?'
10 See the findings of Prof. H. Lauder and his colleagues at Bath University, reported in Brown, P. (2007) 'When merit means nothing', *Times Higher Education Suipplement*, 20 July.

Chapter 11 What is the employers' perspective?

1 Brown, P., Hesketh. A. with Williams, S. (2004) *The mismanagement of talent: employability and jobs in the knowledge economy* (Oxford University Press), Chapter 4 'The war for talent'.
2 Ibid., Chapter 9 'The great training robbery', p. 219.
3 doctorjob.com Student Survey (2003) *A generation betrayed: are graduates disillusioned with the modern job market?* (Wallingford, Oxon: GTI Specialist Publishers).
4 Griffiths, S. (2007) 'Wanted: a degree plus...', *Sunday Times*, Recruitment section, 5 August.
5 Sloane, W. (2007) 'Make the right connection with a click of the mouse', *Sunday Times*, Recruitment section, 5 August, p. 4. Doke, D. (2007) 'Straight to the top of the class', *Sunday Times*, Recruitment section, 5 August.
6 doctorjob.com Student Survey (2003) *A generation betrayed: are graduates disillusioned with the modern job market?* (Wallingford, Oxon: GTI Specialist Publishers).
7 Whitla, D.K. (1975) *Value added: measuring the impact of undergraduate education* (Cambridge, MA: Harvard University, Office of Instructional Research and Evaluation), cited in McClelland, D.C. (1994) 'The Knowledge-Testing-Educational Complex Strikes Back', *American Psychologist*, 49(1), pp. 66–9.
8 Hunter, J.B. and Schmidt, F.L. (1984) 'Validity and utility of alternative predictors of job performance', *Psychological Bulletin*, 96(1), pp. 72–98. Schmidt, F.L. and Hunter, J.B. (1981) 'Employment testing: old theories and new research findings', *American Psychologist*, pp. 1128–36.
9 Sternberg, R.J. (1996) *A more careful view of IQ and job performance* (New York: Simon & Schuster).
10 Feist, G.J. and Barron, F. (1996) 'Emotional intelligence and academic intelligence in career and life success', paper presented at the annual convention of the American Psychological Society, San Francisco.

11 Brown, P., Hesketh. A. with Williams, S. (2004) *The mismanagement of talent: employability and jobs in the knowledge economy* (Oxford University Press), Chapter 4 'The war for talent', pp. 65–88, and Chapter 7 'Picking winners', pp. 147–86.
12 Lipsett, A. (2007) 'Firms turn to psychometric tests to pick graduate recruits', *Education Guardian*, 10 July.
13 Adams, K. (1999) Interview with Daniel Goleman, *Competency*, 6(4), Summer, pp. 33–8.
14 Janovics, C. (2001) 'Emotional intelligence at the work place', paper presented at the 16th annual conference of the Society of Industrial and Organisational Psychology, San Diego.
15 McClelland, D.C. (1973) 'Testing for competence rather than intelligence', *American Psychologist*, 28(1), pp. 1–14.
16 Carnevale, A.P. *et al.* (1989) *Workplace basics: the skills employers want* (US Department of Labor, Employment and Training Administration).
17 Dowd, K.O. and Liedtka, J. (1994) 'What corporations seek in MBA hires: a survey', *Magazine of Graduate Management Admission Council*, Winter.
18 Griffiths, S. (2007) 'Wanted: a degree plus...', *Sunday Times Recruitment*, 5 August. Lipsett, A. (2007) 'Firms turn to psychometric tests to pick graduate recruits', *Education Guardian*, 10 July.
19 Wolf, A. (2002) *Does education matter? Myths about education and economic growth* (London: Penguin), pp. 241–3.
20 Lipsett, A. (2007) 'Firms turn to psychometric tests to pick graduate recruits', *Education Guardian*, 10 July.
21 Brown, P. (2007) 'When merit means nothing', *Times Higher Education Supplement*, 20 July. See also Lauder, H., Brown, P., Dillabough, J.A. and Halsey, A.H. (eds) (2006) *Education, globalization and social change* (Oxford University Press), Part 5 'The family, opportunity and social mobility: the opportunity trap', pp. 381–97.

Chapter 12 Why do so many students make wrong choices?

1 Power, S., Whitty, G. and Edwards, T. (2005) 'Top jobs and highest earnings most likely for elite university graduates', 8 March, HERO [Higher Education Research Opportunities] article ref: 31410, Institute of Education, www.hero.ac.uk/media_relations/8969.cfm
2 Henry, J. (2005) 'Go to a private school and a top college – and add £60,000 to your salary', *Sunday Telegraph*, 6 March.
3 Power, S., Whitty, G. and Edwards, T. (2005) 'Top jobs and highest earnings most likely for elite university graduates', 8 March, HERO [Higher Education Research Opportunities] article ref: 31410, Institute of Education, www.hero.ac.uk/media_relations/8969.cfm
4 Samuelson, R.J. (1999) 'The worthless Ivy League? It's no guarantee of success. Podunk's competent grads will beat Princeton's incompetents', *Newsweek*, 1 November.
5 Krueger, A.B. and Dale, S.B. (1999) 'Better pay for a better college? Not really', *New York Times: Economic Scene*, 27 April.
6 Ibid.
7 Curtis, J. and Attwood, T. (2004) *How students choose universities* (Curtis Associates in association with Hamilton House Mailings Ltd), pp. 12–28.

8   Hill, P. (2005) 'Happy campus tops wish list', *Times Higher Education Supplement*, 17 June.
9   Ibid. See also Hill, P. (2005) 'What impresses today's freshers?', *Times Higher Education Supplement*, 17 June.
10 doctorjob.com Student Survey (2003) *A generation betrayed: are graduates disillusioned with the modern job market?* (Wallingford, Oxon: GTI Specialist Publishers).
11 Utley, A. (2004) '"Bums-on- seats"' policy leads more students to drop out', *Times Higher Education Supplement*, 9 July.
12 Bok, D. (2003) *Universities in the marketplace: the commercialization of higher education* (Princeton and Oxford: Princeton University Press), 160–62.
13 Halpin, T. (2003) 'Most students regret their A-level choices', *The Times*, 13 November.
14 Hill, P. (2005) 'Happy campus tops wish list', *Times Higher Education Supplement*, 17 June.
15 Utley, A. (2004) 'Where to study? Phone a friend', *Times Higher Education Supplement*, 16 January.
16 Ball, C. (2006–07) Higher Education Careers Services Unit, article appearing on prospects.ac.uk, Winter.
17 Utley, A. (2004) 'Where to study? Phone a friend', *Times Higher Education Supplement*, 16 January.
18 Henry, J. (2003) 'Universities seek tomorrow's talent among under-9s', *Sunday Telegraph*, 9 February. Tysome, T. (2007) 'Access agenda is now back on course', *Times Higher Education Supplement*, 20 July.

Chapter 13 Is parent power a reality?

1   Martin, P. (2005) *Making happy people: the nature of happiness and its origins in childhood* (London: Fourth Estate).
2   Martin, P. (2005) 'Being happy is child's play', *Sunday Times*, 6 February.
3   Atkinson, V. (2003) 'How to avoid falling into the parent trap', *Times Higher Education Supplement*, 17 October.
4   [Editorial] (2005) 'Parents must keep out' *Times Higher Education Supplement*, 24 June.
5   Phillips, S. and North, M. (2005) 'Big mother is watching you', *Times Higher Education Supplement*, 24 June.
6   Tysome, T. (2004) 'It's open day – feel free to bring your children', *Times Higher Education Supplement*, 30 July.
7   Fazackerley, A. (2004) 'Furious parents round on Exeter', *Times Higher Education Supplement*, 17 December.Fzackerley

Chapter 14 What can make a difference?

1   Fazackerley, A. (2004) 'Survey: university life is a far cry from stereotype', *Times Higher Education Supplement*, 23 April. See also Astin, A.W. (1993) *What matters in college? Four critical years revisited* (San Francisco: Jossey-Bass), pp. 279–81.
2   Lightfoot, L. (2003) 'Pupils urged to look beyond "trendy" colleges', *Daily Telegraph*, 18 September.
3   Fazackerly, A. (2005) 'North flaunts strengths', *Times Higher Education Supplement*, 5 August.

Conclusion

1   Illich, I. 1970. *Deschooling society* (London: Marion Boyars).
2   Riddell, P. (2003) 'Tories' popularity grows at the expense of Lib Dems', *The Times*, 9 December.
3   Binns, A. (2007) 'Private tuition booms' and 'Fear of growing inequalities as better-off buy extra help', *Times Higher Education Supplement*, 21 September.
4   Lipsett, A. (2006) 'Huge disparity in hours raises question of value', *Times Higher Education Supplement*, 2 November.
5   MacLeod, D. (2007) 'Students in Europe are getting far more hours of tuition than those in the UK', *The Guardian*, EducationGuardian, 25 September. Attwood, R. (2007) 'Part-time effort for full-time degrees', *Times Higher Education Supplement*, 28 September.
6   Baty, P. (2007) 'Private college to award degrees', *Times Higher Education Supplement*, 28 September.
7   Tahir, T. (2007) 'Britain gets vote of foreign students', *Times Higher Education Supplement*, 28 September.
8   Newman, M. (2007) 'Goodbye blue skies?', *Times Higher Education Supplement*, 10 August. [Editorial] (2007) 'Pursuit of truth is paramount', *Times Higher Education Supplement*, 10 August. Baty, P. (2007) 'Research councils to give users more say', *Times Higher Education Supplement*, 12 October. [Editorial] (2007) 'Research must yield more than economic payoff', *Times Higher Education Supplement*, 12 October.
9   Goddard, A. (2004) 'It's not just the economy stupid. Newby justifies expansion plans', *Times Higher Education Supplement*, 2 April.
10 Attwood, R. (2007) 'Fund UK postgrads or lose them, says Cambridge VC', *Times Higher Education Supplement*, 5 October.
11 Attwood, R. (2007) 'Student voice gets Lord's concern', *Times Higher Education Supplement*, 19 October.

Appendix 1 Useful sources of information

1   Langley, W. (2004) 'You can do the job, but can you pass the test?', *Sunday Telegraph*, Review section, 7 November.
2   Doskoch, P. (1998) 'Exhibiting a funny twist of mind', *Psychology Today*, Mar–Apr, review article. See psychologytoday.com/articles/pto-19980301-000049.html